Versatile VEGETABLES

Fresh vegetables are one of our most important foods; they are an essential part of a balanced diet and they taste good. With many people choosing to follow a vegetarian or partly vegetarian diet for their health, and humane and economic reasons, vegetables are becoming the major ingredient of many meals. The availability and variety of vegetables is constantly increasing, but it is worth remembering that the best value vegetables, both for price and taste, are those in season. While this book is not a vegetarian cookbook, it contains many recipes that will appeal to vegetarians.

CONTENTS

THE PANTRY SHELF

Unless otherwise stated, the following ingredients used in this book are:

Cream Double, suitable for whipping
Flour White flour, plain or standard
Sugar White sugar

WHAT'S IN A TABLESPOON?

NEW ZEALAND
1 tablespoon =
15 mL OR 3 teaspoons
UNITED KINGDOM
1 tablespoon =
15 mL OR 3 teaspoons
AUSTRALIA
1 tablespoon =
20 mL OR 4 teaspoons

The recipes in this book were tested in Australia where a 20 mL tablespoon is standard. All measures are level.

The tablespoon in the New Zealand and United Kingdom sets of measuring spoons is 15 mL. In many recipes this difference will not matter. For recipes using baking powder, gelatine, bicarbonate of soda, small quantities of flour and cornflour, simply add another teaspoon for each tablespoon specified.

RECIPE COLLECTION

SOUPS

Vegetable soups are among the quickest, easiest and most economical of soups to make. In this chapter you will find a wonderful collection of vegetable-based soups suitable for one-dish meals and starters. Served with crusty bread or rolls, a soup can be a satisfying main meal.

Curried Lentil Soup, Winter Vegetable Soup

Curried Lentil Soup

2 tablespoons vegetable oil
1 onion, chopped
2 teaspoons curry powder
1/2 teaspoon ground cumin
1 tablespoon tomato paste (purée)
6 cups/1.5 litres/2 1/2 pt vegetable stock
125 g/4 oz red or green lentils
1 small head broccoli, broken into florets
2 carrots, chopped
1 parsnip, chopped
1 stalk celery, chopped
freshly ground black pepper
1 tablespoon chopped fresh parsley

1 Heat oil in a large saucepan, add onion, curry powder and cumin and cook, stirring occasionally, for 4-5 minutes or until onion is soft. Stir in tomato paste (purée) and stock and bring to the boil. Reduce heat, add lentils, cover and simmer for 30 minutes.

2 Add broccoli, carrots, parsnip and celery and cook, covered, for 30 minutes longer or until vegetables are tender. Season to taste with black pepper. Just prior to serving, stir in parsley.

Serves 6

This thick and hearty soup can be made ahead of time and makes a great main meal.

Winter Vegetable Soup

2 tablespoons vegetable oil
1 large onion, sliced
1 clove garlic, crushed
2 stalks celery, chopped
2 carrots, chopped
1 turnip, chopped
440 g/14 oz canned tomatoes, undrained and mashed
2 tablespoons tomato paste (purée)
1 tablespoon finely chopped fresh basil
1 teaspoon dried oregano
1 teaspoon sugar
6 cups/1.5 litres/2 1/2 pt vegetable stock
125 g/4 oz small pasta shells
315 g/10 oz canned red kidney beans, drained and rinsed
freshly ground black pepper

1 Heat oil in a large saucepan, add onion, garlic, celery, carrots and turnip and cook, stirring occasionally, for 4-5 minutes or until vegetables are just tender.

2 Stir in tomatoes, tomato paste (purée), basil, oregano, sugar and stock and bring to the boil. Reduce heat and simmer for 30-45 minutes.

3 Stir in pasta and beans. Season to taste with black pepper and simmer, uncovered, for 30 minutes.

Serves 6

A hearty meal in itself that will satisfy even the hungriest members of your family. Delicious sprinkled with freshly chopped parsley and Parmesan cheese and served with crusty bread.

Zucchini Soup

3 cups/750 mL/1$^1/_4$ pt chicken stock
2 onions, chopped
6 zucchini (courgettes), sliced
$^1/_2$ cup/125 mL/4 fl oz milk
$^1/_2$ cup/125 mL/4 fl oz cream (double)
$^1/_4$ teaspoon ground nutmeg

CURRY PUFFS
$^1/_2$ cup/125 mL/4 fl oz milk
$^1/_2$ teaspoon curry powder
45 g/1$^1/_2$ oz butter
$^2/_3$ cup/75 g/2$^1/_2$ oz flour
1 egg yolk
1 egg

1 Place stock in a large saucepan and bring to the boil. Reduce heat to simmering, add onion and zucchini (courgettes) and simmer for 10 minutes or until vegetables are tender.

2 Using a slotted spoon, remove onion and zucchini (courgettes) from stock and place in a food processor or blender. Add 1 cup/250 mL/8 fl oz stock and process until smooth. Add milk, cream and nutmeg and process for 30 seconds longer.

3 Stir vegetable mixture back into remaining stock and reheat.

4 To make puffs, place milk, curry powder and butter in a small saucepan and bring to the boil over a low heat. Remove pan from heat and stir in flour. Return pan to a low heat and cook for 30 seconds, stirring constantly with a wooden spoon. Remove from heat and set aside to cool for 5 minutes. Place egg yolk and egg in a small bowl and whisk to combine. Slowly add egg mixture to curry mixture, stirring with a wooden spoon until mixture is smooth.

5 Bring a large saucepan of water to the boil, then reduce heat to simmering. Drop teaspoons of curry mixture into water and cook for 5-7 minutes or until puffs float to the top. Remove, using a slotted spoon. To serve, top each bowl of soup with 3-4 puffs.

Serves 4

The Curry Puffs are also delicious with other soups.

Zucchini Soup

Fennel Soup

1 tablespoon olive oil
1 onion, sliced
1 clove garlic, crushed
4 bulbs fennel, trimmed, halved and sliced, feathery tops reserved
440 g/14 oz canned tomatoes, undrained and mashed
1/2 cup/125 mL/4 fl oz tomato paste (purée)
4 cups/1 litre/1 3/4 pt chicken stock
freshly ground black pepper

1 Heat oil in a large saucepan, add onion and garlic and cook, stirring occasionally, for 4-5 minutes or until onion is soft.

2 Add fennel, tomatoes and tomato paste (purée) to pan and cook, stirring occasionally, for 5 minutes.

3 Stir in stock and bring to the boil. Reduce heat, cover and simmer for 30 minutes. Season to taste with black pepper. Serve garnished with reserved fennel tops.

Serves 4

This soup is delicious served with toasted Italian bread. To make, cut Italian bread into thick slices, place on a baking tray and bake at 180°C/350°F/Gas 4 for 10 minutes, turn bread and bake for 10 minutes longer or until golden. Rub hot toast with the cut surface of a clove of garlic. Serve immediately.

Sweet Potato Soup

1 kg/2 lb sweet potatoes, scrubbed
30 g/1 oz butter
2 large leeks, sliced
6 cups/1.5 litres/2 1/2 pt chicken stock
freshly ground black pepper
1/2 cup/125 mL/4 fl oz cream (double)
1/2 bunch/125 g/4 oz watercress, leaves removed and chopped

1 Bake sweet potatoes in their skins for 1 hour or until tender. Set aside until cool enough to handle.

2 Melt butter in a heavy-based saucepan, add leeks and cook over a low heat, stirring, for 5 minutes. Add half the stock, bring to the boil, reduce heat and simmer for 5 minutes or until leeks are tender.

3 Peel sweet potatoes, place flesh in a food processor or blender, add leek mixture and process until smooth. Return sweet potato purée to a clean pan, add remaining stock, bring to the boil, then reduce heat and simmer for 5 minutes. Season to taste with black pepper, set aside to cool, then chill for 3-4 hours or until ready to serve.

4 To serve, ladle soup into chilled bowls, swirl through a little cream and top with chopped watercress.

Serves 6

To speed up the making of this soup, cook the sweet potatoes in the microwave. Cook the sweet potatoes on HIGH (100%), turning several times during cooking, for 15 minutes or until tender.

Chilled Tomato Soup

1 tablespoon olive oil
1 onion, chopped
1 clove garlic, chopped
4 cups/1 litre/1 3/4 pt vegetable stock
4 tablespoons finely chopped fresh mint
440 g/14 oz canned tomatoes, undrained and mashed
2 zucchini (courgettes), coarsely grated
freshly ground black pepper

TOMATO-MINT ICE CUBES
12 fresh mint leaves
3/4 cup/185 mL/6 fl oz tomato juice
3/4 cup/185 mL/6 fl oz water

1 Heat oil in a large saucepan, add onion and garlic and cook, stirring occasionally, for 2-3 minutes or until onion is soft. Add stock and mint and simmer for 5 minutes. Remove pan from heat and set aside to cool.

2 Place tomatoes and stock mixture in a food processor or blender and process until smooth. Stir in zucchini (courgettes) and season to taste with black pepper. Transfer to a large bowl, cover and refrigerate for several hours or until well chilled.

3 To make Tomato-Mint Ice Cubes, place a mint leaf in each space of an ice cube tray. Mix together tomato juice and water, pour into ice cube tray and freeze. To serve, place 3 ice cubes in each soup bowl and pour over chilled soup.

Serves 4

Start a summer dinner party with this low-kilojoule (calorie) easy-to-make refreshing soup. The Tomato-Mint Ice Cubes add a special touch, but plain ice cubes work just as well.

Chicken and Corn Soup

1 large potato, diced
1 large onion, sliced
6 cups/1.5 litres/2 1/2 pt chicken stock
1/2 teaspoon chilli powder, or according to taste
250 g/8 oz cooked chicken, chopped
315 g/10 oz canned sweet corn kernels
2 tablespoons finely chopped fresh parsley
freshly ground black pepper

1 Place potato, onion, stock and chilli powder in a large saucepan and bring to the boil. Reduce heat and simmer for 20 minutes or until vegetables are tender.

2 Remove vegetables from stock and place in a food processor or blender and process until smooth. Return vegetable purée to stock and whisk to combine. Stir in chicken and sweet corn and cook over a low heat, stirring occasionally, for 10 minutes or until soup is heated through. Stir in parsley and season to taste with black pepper.

Serves 6

Using a vegetable purée is a great way to thicken soups without adding thickeners laden with kilojoules (calories). This method can be used for any soup containing vegetables such as potatoes, pumpkin or sweet potatoes.

Chilled Tomato Soup,
Chicken and Corn Soup

Green Minestrone

60 g/2 oz butter
250 g/8 oz asparagus, stalks chopped, tips reserved
250 g/8 oz broccoli, broken into florets
6 spring onions, chopped
250 g/8 oz fresh or frozen broad beans
250 g/8 oz fresh or frozen peas
4 cups/1 litre/$1^3/4$ pt chicken stock
250 g/8 oz green beans, cut into 2.5 cm/1 in pieces
freshly ground black pepper

1 Melt butter in a large saucepan, add asparagus stalks, broccoli, spring onions, broad beans and 185 g/6 oz peas and cook, stirring, for 5 minutes.

2 Stir in stock and bring to the boil. Reduce heat and simmer for 15 minutes or until vegetables are tender. Using a slotted spoon, transfer vegetables to a food processor or blender and process until smooth.

3 Return vegetable purée to stock mixture. Add reserved asparagus tips, green beans and remaining peas and bring to the boil. Reduce heat and simmer for 5 minutes or until vegetables are tender. Season to taste with black pepper.

Serves 4

Most soups freeze well. When freezing any liquid leave a 5 cm/2 in space between the soup and lid of the container, as liquid expands during freezing.

Left: Creamy Mushroom Soup
Far left: Green Minestrone

Creamy Mushroom Soup

90 g/3 oz butter
1 large onion, sliced
250 g/8 oz button mushrooms, sliced
1 tablespoon chopped fresh chervil or parsley
2 cups/500 mL/16 fl oz chicken stock
2 tablespoons cornflour
1 cup/250 mL/8 fl oz milk
$^{1}/_{2}$ cup/125 mL/8 fl oz cream (double)

1 Melt butter in a large saucepan, add onion and mushrooms and cook, stirring, over a medium heat for 5 minutes.

2 Stir in chervil or parsley and stock and bring to the boil. Reduce heat and simmer for 20 minutes. Using a slotted spoon transfer onion and mushrooms to a food processor or blender and process until smooth. Return vegetable purée to stock mixture.

3 Combine cornflour with $^{1}/_{4}$ cup/ 60 mL/2 fl oz milk, then blend in remaining milk. Stir milk mixture into soup and cook over a medium heat, stirring constantly, until soup thickens slightly. Stir in cream and heat over a low heat for 2-3 minutes or until soup is heated through.

Serves 4

Serve this soup garnished with a sprig of fresh chervil or parsley and lightly cooked sliced mushrooms.

STARTERS

A first course based on vegetables makes a light and healthy start to a meal. In this chapter you will find recipes such as Asparagus Stir-Fry and Crispy Artichokes which show off tasty vegetables at their best.

Crudités with Herb Dip

Crudites with Herb Dip

a selection of vegetables, such as broccoli and cauliflower florets, carrot sticks and baby new potatoes

HERB DIP
2 tablespoons chopped fresh parsley
2 tablespoons chopped fresh basil
1/2 cup/125 g/4 oz mayonnaise
1/3 cup/90 g/3 oz sour cream
2 teaspoons Dijon mustard
freshly ground black pepper

1 Steam or microwave vegetables separately until just tender. Drain, refresh under cold running water, drain again and set aside.

2 To make dip, place parsley, basil, mayonnaise, sour cream, mustard and black pepper to taste in a food processor or blender and process to combine.

3 To serve, arrange vegetables on a large platter and accompany with dip.

Serves 10

This dip is delicious served with any lightly cooked or steamed vegetables. You might like to try serving snow peas (mangetout), zucchini (courgettes), asparagus or cucumber on this platter instead of, or as well as, the vegetables that are suggested in the recipe.

Asparagus Stir-Fry

1 tablespoon vegetable oil
2 teaspoons sesame oil
1 tablespoon chopped fresh ginger
750 g/1 1/2 lb asparagus spears, cut into 4 cm/1 1/2 in pieces
60 g/2 oz roughly chopped roasted cashews
1 tablespoon soy sauce

1 Heat vegetable and sesame oils together in a wok or frying pan. Add ginger and stir-fry for 1 minute.

2 Add asparagus and stir-fry for 4-5 minutes or until asparagus is tender crisp and bright green. Stir in cashews and soy sauce and stir-fry for 1-2 minutes longer. Serve immediately.

Serves 6 as a starter

Green beans are also delicious cooked in this way.

'Asparagus was cultivated and enjoyed by Roman epicures as early as 200 BC.'

Baked Asparagus Roll-Ups

Oven temperature
200°C, 400°F, Gas 6

If fresh asparagus is unavailable make this recipe using well-drained canned asparagus.

28 asparagus spears, trimmed
14 slices thin wholemeal bread, crusts removed
250 g/8 oz cream cheese
1/2 teaspoon prepared hot English mustard
100 g/3 1/2 oz finely chopped ham
125 g/4 oz butter, melted

1 Boil, steam or microwave asparagus until just tender. Refresh under cold running water. Drain well and set aside.

2 Flatten bread slices using a rolling pin. Place cream cheese, mustard and ham in a bowl and mix to combine. Spread cream cheese mixture over each slice of bread.

3 Arrange 2 asparagus spears on each slice of bread with tips towards outside edges. Roll up, cut each roll in half and secure with a toothpick. Place rolls seam side down on a baking tray lined with nonstick baking paper.

4 Brush rolls with butter and bake for 15-20 minutes or until lightly browned.

Makes 28

Asparagus Pastries

Oven temperature
220°C, 425°F, Gas 7

This hollandaise sauce can be quickly and easily made in the microwave. To make, place egg yolks, lemon juice and orange juice in a microwave-safe jug or bowl and whisk to combine. Whisk in melted butter and cook on MEDIUM (50%), stirring every 30 seconds, for 1 1/2 minutes or until sauce thickens.

155 g/5 oz prepared puff pastry
1 egg yolk, lightly beaten
18 asparagus spears, trimmed

ORANGE HOLLANDAISE SAUCE
3 egg yolks
1 tablespoon lemon juice
2 tablespoons orange juice
125 g/4 oz butter, melted

1 Roll out pastry thinly and cut into twelve rectangles, each 5 x 10 cm/2 x 4 in. Place pastry rectangles on a baking tray lined with nonstick baking paper, brush with egg yolk and bake for 10-15 minutes or until pastry is puffed and golden.

2 Boil, steam or microwave asparagus until tender. Drain, set aside and keep warm.

3 To make sauce, place egg yolks, lemon juice and orange juice in a food processor or blender and process until light and fluffy. With machine running, slowly pour in butter.

4 Place sauce in a bowl, set over a saucepan of simmering water and cook, stirring constantly, until sauce thickens. To serve, arrange 3 asparagus spears on half the pastry rectangles, spoon over sauce and top with remaining pastry rectangles.

Serves 6

Asparagus Pastries,
Asparagus Ginger Stir-Fry,
Baked Asparagus Roll-Ups

Right: Pâté-filled Mushrooms
Below: Tzatziki

TZATZIKI

This easy dip makes a refreshing start to a meal and is also delicious served with raw vegetables.

1 large cucumber, peeled and grated
500 g/1 lb natural yogurt
1 tablespoon chopped fresh mint
1 tablespoon chopped fresh parsley
2 cloves garlic, crushed
freshly ground black pepper
2 French breadsticks

1 Place cucumber, yogurt, mint, parsley, garlic and black pepper to taste in a bowl and mix to combine. Cover and refrigerate for at least 1 hour or until required.

2 To serve, accompany Tzatziki with broken or sliced bread for dipping.

Serves 8

Pate-filled Mushrooms

8 large mushrooms, stalks removed
125 g/4 oz rashers bacon, chopped

CHICKEN LIVER PATE
90 g/2 oz butter
250 g/8 oz chicken livers, cleaned
4 tablespoons port
freshly ground black pepper

1 To make pâté, melt butter in a frying pan, add chicken livers and cook over a medium heat, stirring, for 2 minutes. Add port and black pepper to taste and cook for 5 minutes longer.

2 Remove pan from heat and set aside to cool for 10 minutes. Transfer chicken livers and pan juices to a food processor or blender and process until smooth.

3 Spoon a little pâté mixture into each mushroom cap, sprinkle with bacon, place on a baking tray and bake for 15 minutes or until bacon is cooked.

Serves 4

Oven temperature
180°C, 350°F, Gas 4

For a speedy version of this dish you can use purchased pâté.

ARTICHOKE SAVOURIES

Oven temperature
200°C, 400°F, Gas 6

12 slices bread
3 tablespoons vegetable oil
1/4 cup/60 g/2 oz mayonnaise
1 tablespoon cream (double)
1 tablespoon snipped fresh chives
freshly ground black pepper
2 tablespoons finely chopped red pepper
440 g/14 oz canned artichoke hearts, drained and halved
12 sprigs fresh dill

1 Using a 5 cm/2 in biscuit cutter, cut out 12 circles of bread. Brush both sides of each bread circle with a little oil and place on a baking tray lined with nonstick baking paper and bake for 10-15 minutes or until bread is golden and toasted.

2 Place mayonnaise, cream, chives and black pepper to taste in a small bowl and mix to combine.

3 To assemble, top each bread circle with half an artichoke heart, a spoonful of mayonnaise mixture, a little red pepper and a sprig of dill. Serve immediately.

Makes 12

For these savouries, the toast rounds and the mayonnaise can be made in advance, but leave the assembly until just prior to serving or the toast will go soggy.

Left: Artichoke Savouries
Below: Crispy Artichokes

Crispy Artichokes

3 artichokes
1 cup/60 g/2 oz breadcrumbs, made from stale bread
125 g/4 oz grated fresh Parmesan cheese
4 eggs, lightly beaten
1 cup/250 mL/8 fl oz olive oil

1 Remove and discard tough outside leaves of artichokes. Bring a large saucepan of water to the boil, add artichokes and boil for 30 minutes or until tender. Remove artichokes from water, drain and set aside to cool.

2 Remove leaves from cooked artichokes, leaving hearts intact. Set leaves aside and cut hearts into quarters.

3 Place breadcrumbs and Parmesan cheese in a bowl and mix to combine. Dip bottom half of leaves into egg mixture then into breadcrumb mixture. Dip hearts into egg mixture then into breadcrumb mixture to coat completely.

4 Heat oil in a large frying pan until a cube of bread dropped in browns in 50 seconds. Cook leaves and hearts a few at a time until golden and crisp. Drain on absorbent kitchen paper and serve immediately.

Serves 6

You may have wondered why artichokes are often served at the beginning of a meal. It's because they contain a milky substance which has a peculiar effect on the taste of wine. If serving artichokes at a dinner party, serve the artichokes first then the wine, so you and your guests can appreciate both.

Main Meals

While many of the meals in this chapter are suitable for vegetarians, some of them also include small amounts of meat or fish, making them perfect for those choosing to eat smaller quantities of these foods.

Savoury Pumpkin Flan

Savoury Pumpkin Flan

4 sheets filo pastry
2 tablespoons vegetable oil
2 rashers bacon, chopped
1 onion, chopped
250 g/8 oz pumpkin or carrots, cooked and mashed
185 g/6 oz grated tasty cheese (mature Cheddar)
2 eggs, separated
2 tablespoons sour cream or natural yogurt
pinch chilli powder
freshly ground black pepper
1 tablespoon chopped fresh parsley

1 Brush each sheet of pastry with oil and fold in half. Layer pastry, one folded piece on top of the other to give eight layers. Place an 18 cm/7 in flan dish upside down on layered pastry and cut around dish, making a circle 3 cm/1¼ in larger. Lift all layers of pastry into dish and roll edges.

2 Cook bacon and onion in a frying pan for 4-5 minutes or until bacon is cooked and crisp. Place pumpkin or carrots, cheese, egg yolks, sour cream or yogurt, chilli powder and black pepper to taste in a bowl and mix to combine.

3 Place egg whites in a bowl and beat until stiff peaks form. Fold egg white mixture into pumpkin mixture and spoon into pastry case. Sprinkle pumpkin mixture with parsley and bake for 30 minutes or until pastry is golden and cooked.

Serves 4

Oven temperature
200°C, 400°F, Gas 6

When incorporating beaten egg whites into a mixture, first stir in 1 tablespoon of beaten egg white, then lightly fold remaining beaten egg white through, working as quickly as possible.

Mushroom Gougere

CHOUX PASTRY
1 cup/250 mL/8 fl oz water
90 g/3 oz butter
1 cup/125 g/4 oz flour, sifted
4 eggs

MUSHROOM FILLING
155 g/5 oz button mushrooms, sliced
3 eggs, lightly beaten
155 g/5 oz sour cream
½ cup/125 mL/4 fl oz cream (double)
1 tablespoon flour
125 g/4 oz grated tasty cheese (mature Cheddar)
1 tablespoon chopped fresh parsley
pinch ground nutmeg
freshly ground black pepper

1 To make pastry, place water and butter in a saucepan, cover and cook until butter melts and mixture just boils. Remove pan from heat and add flour all at once. Stir vigorously with a wooden spoon over a low heat until mixture forms a ball and pulls away from sides of pan. Set aside to cool slightly.

2 Add eggs one at a time, beating well after each addition until mixture is smooth and glossy. Spread mixture around sides of a greased shallow 23 cm/9 in ovenproof dish.

3 To make filling, place mushrooms, eggs, sour cream, cream, flour, cheese, parsley, nutmeg and black pepper to taste in a bowl and mix to combine. Spoon filling into centre of pastry and bake for 35-40 minutes or until filling is firm and pastry is puffed and golden.

Serves 4

Oven temperature
200°C, 400°F, Gas 6

Mushrooms should be stored in a brown paper bag or a cloth bag in the refrigerator. Stored in this way they will keep fresh for 5-7 days. Never store mushrooms in a plastic bag as this causes them to sweat and deteriorate very quickly.

Spinach and Basil Risotto

1 bunch/500 g/1 lb spinach, stalks removed and leaves chopped
1 cup/250 mL/8 fl oz water
60 g/2 oz butter
1 large onion, finely chopped
2 cloves garlic, crushed
2 cups/440 g/14 oz brown rice
1/2 cup/125 mL/4 fl oz white wine
5 cups/1.2 litres/2 pt hot chicken stock
30 g/1 oz fresh basil leaves
2 tablespoons olive oil
4 tablespoons pine nuts, toasted

1 Place spinach and water in a saucepan, bring to the boil and cook for 1 minute or until spinach is tender. Remove from heat and set aside to cool.

2 Place spinach mixture in a food processor or blender and process until smooth. Set aside.

3 Melt butter in a saucepan, add onion and garlic and cook for 4-5 minutes or until onion is soft. Add rice to pan and stir to coat with butter mixture. Pour in wine and half the chicken stock. Cook over a medium heat, stirring occasionally, until almost all the liquid is absorbed. Stir in remaining stock with reserved spinach mixture and cook until almost all the liquid is absorbed.

4 Place basil, oil and 3 tablespoons pine nuts in food processor or blender and process until smooth. Stir into rice mixture. Sprinkle with remaining pine nuts and serve immediately.

Serves 4

Risotto is an Italian favourite. Wonderful as a first course, main course or an accompaniment to meat, fish or poultry, it is nutritious and easy to make.

Wholemeal Spinach Quiche

Oven temperature
220°C, 425°F, Gas 7

155 g/5 oz prepared wholemeal pastry

SPINACH FILLING
30 g/1 oz butter
1 onion, finely chopped
1/2 bunch/250 g/8 oz spinach, stalks removed and leaves finely shredded
3 eggs, lightly beaten
300 g/9 1/2 oz sour cream
60 g/2 oz grated tasty cheese (mature Cheddar)
pinch ground nutmeg
freshly ground black pepper

1 Roll out pastry and line the base and sides of a lightly greased 23 cm/9 in flan tin. Trim edges of pastry and line base with baking paper. Fill with uncooked rice and bake for 15 minutes. Remove rice and paper and bake for 10 minutes longer. Remove from oven and set aside to cool slightly.

2 To make filling, melt butter in a frying pan, add onion and cook over a medium heat for 4-5 minutes or until soft. Stir in spinach and cook for 2-3 minutes longer or until spinach wilts. Remove pan from heat and set aside.

3 Place eggs, sour cream, cheese, nutmeg and black pepper to taste in a bowl and mix to combine. Spread spinach mixture over base of pastry case, then carefully spoon in egg mixture. Reduce oven temperature to 180°C/350°F/Gas 4 and bake for 30 minutes or until filling is firm.

Serves 6

When making pastry, have all the utensils and ingredients as cold as possible. In hot weather, chill the utensils before using. Wash your hands in cold water and use only your fingertips for kneading.

*Mushroom Gougère,
Wholemeal Spinach Quiche,
Spinach and Basil Risotto*

Chilli and Chicken Peppers

Oven temperature
200°C, 400°F, Gas 6

If you can find different-coloured peppers this dish will look spectacular, but using only one variety makes no difference to the delicious taste. Leftover Christmas turkey is ideal to use in place of chicken.

3 red peppers
2 green peppers

CHILLI AND CHICKEN FILLING

1 tablespoon vegetable oil
2 spring onions, finely chopped
1 clove garlic, crushed
1 cooked chicken, skinned, flesh removed and chopped
250 g/8 oz cream cheese, softened
1 teaspoon chilli sauce, or according to taste
2 eggs, lightly beaten
60 g/2 oz grated tasty cheese (mature Cheddar)
freshly ground black pepper
60 g/2 oz grated mozzarella cheese
paprika

1 Cut tops from peppers and reserve. Remove seeds and cores. Dice one red pepper and reserved tops. Blanch remaining four pepper shells in boiling water for 2 minutes. Drain upside down on absorbent kitchen paper.

2 To make filling, heat oil in a frying pan, add diced pepper, spring onions and garlic and cook for 4-5 minutes or until pepper is soft. Place chicken, cream cheese, chilli sauce, eggs and tasty cheese (mature Cheddar) in a bowl and mix to combine. Add onion mixture and season to taste with black pepper.

3 Spoon filling into prepared pepper shells and sprinkle with mozzarella cheese and paprika.

4 Place filled peppers close together in a shallow baking dish and bake for 30-40 minutes or until filling is bubbling hot and cheese is golden.

Serves 4

Chilli and Chicken Peppers

Vegetables in Pitta Baskets

Vegetables in Pitta Baskets

vegetable oil for deep-frying
2 large pitta bread rounds, split through centre

VEGETABLE FILLING

8 baby new potatoes, cut into bite-sized pieces
1 carrot, chopped
1 zucchini (courgette), chopped
250 g/8 oz snow peas (mangetout)
250 g/8 oz green or yellow baby squash, quartered
1 tablespoon grated fresh ginger
2 tablespoons honey
2 tablespoons orange juice
2 tablespoons chopped macadamia or brazil nuts
2 tablespoons snipped fresh chives

1 Heat oil in a wok or large saucepan until a cube of bread dropped in browns in 50 seconds. Cook pitta breads one at a time, pressing with the head of a metal soup ladle to form a basket. Drain on absorbent kitchen paper. Set aside and keep warm.

2 To make filling, boil, steam or microwave potatoes, carrot, zucchini (courgette), snow peas (mangetout) and squash, separately, until tender. Set aside and keep warm.

3 Place ginger, honey, orange juice, nuts and chives in a large bowl and mix to combine. Add warm vegetables and toss to coat. Spoon vegetable mixture into warm baskets and serve immediately.

Serves 4

These pitta baskets make wonderful containers for serving all kinds of food. You might like to try them with curried vegetables or meat. If baby squash are not available use sliced zucchini (courgettes) instead.

STEAK AND VEGETABLE SALAD

Oven temperature
180°C, 350°F, Gas 4

1/2 cup/125 mL/4 fl oz olive oil
500 g/1 lb piece rump steak
1 eggplant (aubergine), cut into thick strips
1 onion, sliced
60 g/2 oz pine nuts
250 g/8 oz cherry tomatoes, halved

PESTO DRESSING
1 bunch fresh basil, leaves removed
2 cloves garlic, crushed
1/4 cup/60 mL/2 fl oz olive oil
2 tablespoons white wine vinegar
1 egg yolk
freshly ground black pepper

1 Heat 2 tablespoons oil in a large frying pan, add steak and cook for 3-4 minutes each side or until brown. Transfer to a baking dish and bake for 15 minutes or until cooked to your liking. Cut steak into thin strips and set aside to cool.

2 Heat remaining oil in a frying pan, add eggplant (aubergine), onion and pine nuts and cook, stirring constantly, for 5 minutes or until eggplant (aubergine) is tender. Remove pan from heat, add steak and toss to combine.

3 To make dressing, place basil leaves, garlic, oil, vinegar, egg yolk and black pepper to taste in a food processor or blender and process until smooth.

4 To serve, arrange steak mixture and tomatoes on a serving platter or individual plates and drizzle over dressing.

Serves 4

For a complete meal, serve this salad with Potato and Pepper Salad (see following recipe).

POTATO AND PEPPER SALAD

750 g/1 1/2 lb baby new potatoes, scrubbed
1/2 cup/125 mL/4 fl oz olive oil
3 tablespoons white wine
1 tablespoon red wine vinegar
1 teaspoon crushed black peppercorns
1 red pepper, cut into thin strips
1 green pepper, cut into thin strips
2 cloves garlic, crushed

1 Boil or microwave potatoes until tender. Drain and set aside.

2 Place 4 tablespoons oil, wine, vinegar and black peppercorns in a bowl and whisk to combine. Add warm potatoes, toss to coat potatoes with dressing and set aside.

3 Heat remaining oil in a frying pan, add red pepper, green pepper and garlic and cook over a medium heat, stirring constantly, for 3-4 minutes. Add pepper mixture to potato mixture and toss to combine. Serve warm.

Serves 4

Potatoes have many uses besides being a food. For example, if you accidentally oversalt a casserole or stew, simply place three or four thick slices of potato in the oversalted food and cook until the excess salt has been absorbed by the potato. Remove the potato slices and discard.

Potato and Pepper Salad,
Steak and Vegetable Salad

Broccoli and Cheese Terrine

Oven temperature
200°C, 400°F, Gas 6

500 g/1 lb broccoli, cut into florets
15 g/$^1/_2$ oz butter
1 onion, finely chopped
2 eggs, separated
1 tablespoon chopped fresh parsley
1 tablespoon snipped fresh chives
250 g/8 oz cottage cheese
3 slices multigrain bread, crumbed
3 tablespoons grated Parmesan cheese
3 tablespoons grated tasty cheese (mature Cheddar)
freshly ground black pepper

1 Boil, steam or microwave broccoli until tender. Drain, refresh under cold running water and set aside.

2 Melt butter in a frying pan, add onion and cook, stirring, for 4-5 minutes or until onion is soft.

3 Place broccoli, onion, egg yolks, parsley, chives and cottage cheese in a food processor or blender and process until smooth. Transfer broccoli mixture to a bowl, add crumbed bread, Parmesan cheese, tasty cheese (mature Cheddar) and black pepper to taste and mix to combine. Place egg whites in a bowl and beat until stiff peaks form. Fold egg mixture into broccoli mixture

4 Spoon broccoli mixture into a greased and lined 11 x 21 cm/4$^1/_2$ x 8$^1/_2$ in loaf tin and bake for 25 minutes or until set. Allow to cool for 5 minutes before cutting into slices to serve.

Serves 6

For a complete meal, serve this terrine with a fresh tomato sauce and accompany with a tossed mixed vegetable salad.

Left: Broccoli and Cheese Terrine
Below: Sweet Corn and Prawn Salad

Sweet Corn and Prawn Salad

440 g/14 oz canned sweet corn kernels, drained
1 onion, finely chopped
250 g/8 oz cooked prawns, shelled, deveined and cut into 1 cm/$^1/_2$ in pieces
2 tomatoes, chopped
4 spring onions, chopped
1 red pepper, finely chopped

RED WINE VINEGAR DRESSING
2 tablespoons red wine vinegar
2 tablespoons olive oil
1 clove garlic, crushed
1 tablespoon lemon juice
freshly ground black pepper

1 Place sweet corn, onion, prawns, tomatoes, spring onions and red pepper in a bowl.

2 To make dressing, place vinegar, oil, garlic, lemon juice and black pepper to taste in a screwtop jar and shake well to combine. Spoon dressing over salad and toss to combine.

Serves 4

Fresh sweet corn could be used for this salad if you wish. To remove whole kernels from a cob, blanch the cob in boiling water for 5 minutes, then remove from the water, hold upright and using a sharp knife and cutting downwards remove kernels close to the cob.

Vegetable Lasagne

Oven temperature
180°C, 350°F, Gas 4

As an accompaniment to this hearty lasagne choose a light salad or mixed steamed vegetables.

1 tablespoon olive oil
$^{1}/_{2}$ teaspoon crushed black peppercorns
3 tablespoons lemon juice
1 large eggplant (aubergine), halved lengthwise and cut into 5 mm/$^{1}/_{4}$ in slices
$^{1}/_{2}$ cup/30 g/1 oz wholemeal breadcrumbs, made from stale bread
3 tablespoons grated Parmesan cheese
1 large onion, chopped
2 cloves garlic, crushed
440 g/14 oz canned tomatoes, drained, chopped and 1 tablespoon juice reserved
$^{3}/_{4}$ cup/185 mL/6 fl oz tomato purée
2 tablespoons white wine
1 teaspoon dried oregano
1 teaspoon dried basil
pinch cayenne pepper
6 sheets instant (no precooking required) wholemeal lasagne
185 g/6 oz ricotta cheese
3 tablespoons grated mozzarella cheese

1 Combine olive oil, black peppercorns and lemon juice and brush over eggplant (aubergine) slices. Cook eggplant (aubergine) under a preheated medium grill for 3-4 minutes each side or until golden. Set aside.

2 Place breadcrumbs and Parmesan cheese in a bowl, mix to combine and set aside.

3 Heat a nonstick frying pan, add onion, garlic and reserved tomato juice and cook over a medium heat, stirring, for 5 minutes or until onion is soft. Add tomatoes, tomato purée, wine, oregano, basil and cayenne pepper and cook for 5 minutes longer.

4 Spread one-third of the tomato mixture over base of a 15 x 25 cm/6 x 10 in ovenproof dish. Top with 3 lasagne sheets, half the breadcrumb mixture and cover with a layer of eggplant (aubergine). Top with half the ricotta cheese. Repeat layers, ending with a layer of tomato mixture. Sprinkle with mozzarella cheese and bake for 45 minutes.

Serves 6

Vegetable Lasagne

Fish and Vegetable Curry

2 tablespoons vegetable oil
1 clove garlic, crushed
1 teaspoon yellow mustard seeds
3 tablespoons blanched whole almonds
1 tablespoon curry paste
1 tablespoon chopped lemon grass or 2 teaspoons finely grated lemon rind
750 g/1 1/2 lb boneless white fish fillets, cut into strips
1/3 cup/90 mL/3 fl oz coconut milk
440 g/14 oz asparagus or green beans, cut into 5 cm/2 in pieces
freshly ground black pepper

1 Heat oil in a large frying pan or wok, add garlic, mustard seeds and almonds and stir-fry over a medium heat for 3-4 minutes or until almonds are golden. Stir in curry paste and cook for 3 minutes.

2 Add lemon grass or lemon rind and fish and stir-fry for 3-4 minutes or until fish is almost cooked. Add coconut milk, asparagus or beans and black pepper to taste. Stir-fry for 3 minutes longer or until asparagus is just cooked. Serve immediately.

Serves 6

If commercially made coconut milk is unavailable, you can make your own. To make coconut milk, place 500 g/1 lb desiccated coconut in a bowl and pour over 3 cups/750 mL/1 1/4 pt boiling water. Leave to stand for 30 minutes then strain, squeezing the coconut to extract as much liquid as possible. This will make a thick coconut milk. The coconut can be used again to make a weaker coconut milk.

Roasted Pepper Quiches

500 g/1 lb prepared shortcrust pastry
3 tablespoons grated Parmesan cheese

RED PEPPER FILLING
15 g/1/2 oz butter
1 onion, finely sliced
2 eggs
3/4 cup/185 mL/6 fl oz cream (single)
freshly ground black pepper
1 red pepper, roasted and skin removed
2 tomatoes, peeled, seeded and chopped
1 tablespoon finely chopped fresh basil

1 Roll out pastry and line base and sides of six lightly greased individual flan dishes. Line pastry cases with nonstick baking paper, fill with uncooked rice and bake for 10 minutes. Reduce oven temperature to 180°C/350°F/Gas 4, remove rice and paper and bake for 10-15 minutes longer or until pastry is lightly browned. Set aside to cool.

2 To make filling, melt butter in a small frying pan, add onion and cook over a medium heat for 5-6 minutes or until onion is soft. Place eggs, cream and black pepper to taste in a bowl and whisk to combine.

3 Cut red pepper into 1 cm/1/2 in squares and set aside. Place red pepper, tomatoes, basil and onion mixture in a bowl and toss to combine. Divide red pepper mixture between pastry cases, spoon over egg mixture and sprinkle with Parmesan cheese. Bake at 180°C/350°F/Gas 4 for 15-20 minutes or until filling is firm.

Serves 6

Oven temperature
200°C, 400°F, Gas 6

To roast peppers, place them under a preheated grill and leave until skins char and blister. Alternatively, place them in the oven at 220°C/425°F/Gas 7 and bake for 20-30 minutes or until skin blisters and chars. Once the peppers are roasted, place them in a paper or freezer bag and leave for about 10 minutes or until cool enough to handle. The skins will then slip off and the peppers will be ready to use.

RECIPE COLLECTION

Vegetarian

Vegetarians are in for a treat when they try the recipes in this chapter – both the committed and the occasional vegetarian will be inspired.

Vegetable Pasta Bake

Vegetable Pasta Bake

9 sheets instant (no precooking required) wholemeal lasagne
250 g/8 oz tofu, beaten until smooth

VEGETABLE FILLING
1 tablespoon olive oil
1/4 small cabbage, shredded
1 carrot, finely chopped
1 large green pepper, finely chopped
1 large red pepper, finely chopped
315 g/10 oz canned sweet corn kernels, drained
440 g/14 oz canned tomatoes, undrained and mashed
5 tablespoons chopped fresh basil
freshly ground black pepper

CHEESY TOPPING
125 g/4 oz grated mozzarella cheese
1/2 cup/30 g/1 oz wholemeal breadcrumbs, made from stale bread
4 tablespoons chopped walnuts

1 To make filling, heat oil in a saucepan, add cabbage, carrot, green pepper, red pepper, sweet corn, tomatoes and basil and cook over a medium heat, stirring frequently, until boiling. Reduce heat and simmer for 15 minutes or until vegetables are soft and mixture reduces and thickens. Season to taste with black pepper.

2 To make topping, combine cheese, breadcrumbs and walnuts. Set aside.

3 Spread one-third of filling over base of a lightly greased ovenproof dish, cover with a layer of lasagne sheets and spread with 90 g/3 oz tofu, then with one-third of filling. Repeat layers, finishing with a layer of lasagne sheets. Spread with remaining tofu, sprinkle with topping and bake for 30-35 minutes or until lasagne sheets are tender.

Serves 6

Oven temperature
180°C, 350°F, Gas 4

A lighter version of lasagne, this delicious dish uses instant lasagne and does not have the heavy sauce of traditional lasagne.
You might like to use ricotta cheese in place of tofu in the recipe.

Oriental Toss

3 celery stalks, cut into thin strips
3 carrots, cut into thin strips
3 zucchini (courgettes), cut into thin strips
2 large leeks, cut into thin strips
1 parsnip, cut into thin strips
125 g/4 oz bean sprouts
2 tablespoons vegetable oil
1 onion, sliced
1 tablespoon cornflour blended with 2 tablespoons water
3 tablespoons sesame seeds, toasted

TERIYAKI MARINADE
1 teaspoon grated fresh ginger
2 cloves garlic, crushed
1/4 cup/60 mL/2 fl oz dry sherry
1/2 cup/125 mL/4 fl oz teriyaki sauce
4 tablespoons honey, warmed

1 To make marinade, combine ginger, garlic, sherry, teriyaki sauce and honey. Add celery, carrots, zucchini (courgettes), leeks, parsnip and bean sprouts and toss. Cover and refrigerate for 1 hour.

2 Heat oil in a wok or large frying pan, add onion and cook for 4-5 minutes. Drain vegetables and reserve marinade. Add vegetables to pan and stir-fry for 5 minutes or until vegetables are just tender.

3 Combine half the reserved marinade with cornflour mixture and stir into vegetables. Bring to the boil, reduce heat and simmer until sauce thickens slightly. Sprinkle with sesame seeds and serve.

Serves 6

For a complete meal, serve this stir-fry on a bed of egg noodles.

Fettuccine with Mushrooms

500 g/1 lb fettuccine
1 tablespoon olive oil
2 tablespoons grated Parmesan cheese
2 tablespoons snipped fresh chives

MUSHROOM SAUCE
1 tablespoon olive oil
1 large onion, sliced
2 cloves garlic, crushed
500 g/1 lb button mushrooms, sliced
15 g/1/2 oz butter
1 tablespoon flour
1/4 cup/60 mL/2 fl oz white wine
1 cup/250 mL/8 fl oz vegetable stock
1/2 cup/125 mL/4 fl oz cream (single)
2 tablespoons chopped fresh basil
freshly ground black pepper

Easy enough for a family meal, yet special enough for easy entertaining, this is the perfect way to serve fettuccine when time is short.

1 Cook fettuccine in boiling water in a large saucepan, following packet directions. Drain, toss in oil, set aside and keep warm.

2 To make sauce, heat oil in a saucepan, add onion and garlic and cook for 10 minutes or until onion is golden. Stir in mushrooms and cook for 5 minutes longer. Remove from pan and drain on absorbent kitchen paper.

3 Melt butter in a clean saucepan. Mix in flour and cook for 2 minutes. Remove pan from heat and gradually stir in wine and stock. Cook, stirring constantly, until sauce boils and thickens. Whisk in cream and stir in mushroom mixture and basil. Season to taste with black pepper and cook over a low heat until heated. To serve, spoon sauce over hot pasta and top with Parmesan cheese and chives.

Serves 6

Spinach Pie

Oven temperature
200°C, 400°F, Gas 6

8 spinach leaves, stalks removed and leaves shredded
30 g/1 oz butter
1 onion, finely chopped
1/2 cup/125 g/4 oz ricotta cheese
125 g/4 oz feta cheese, crumbled
60 g/2 oz grated tasty cheese (mature Cheddar)
3 tablespoons grated Parmesan cheese
4 eggs, lightly beaten
1/4 teaspoon ground nutmeg
freshly ground black pepper
8 sheets filo pastry
3 tablespoons olive oil

Serve this quick-to-prepare pie hot or cold. Any leftovers are great to put in school or office lunch boxes.

1 Boil, steam or microwave spinach until just tender. Drain and cool completely, then squeeze to remove excess liquid. Chop spinach finely and place in a bowl.

2 Melt butter in a frying pan, add onion and cook for 4-5 minutes. Combine spinach, onion, ricotta cheese, feta cheese, tasty cheese (mature Cheddar) and Parmesan cheese. In a separate bowl, place eggs, nutmeg and black pepper to taste and whisk to combine. Fold egg mixture into spinach mixture.

3 Layer 4 sheets of pastry together, brushing between each sheet with oil. Repeat with remaining sheets. Line a deep, lightly greased ovenproof dish with a pastry layer. Trim edges about 2.5 cm/1 in from edge of dish. Spoon in spinach mixture, then fold remaining pastry layer in half and place on top of spinach filling. Gently fold edges of pastry together, brush top of pie with oil and bake for 40-45 minutes.

Serves 8

Spinach Pie, Oriental Toss, Fettuccine with Mushrooms

Right: Marinated Tofu Salad
Below: Spicy Rice and Vegetables

SPICY RICE AND VEGETABLES

This dish is easily cooked in the microwave. Place oil, onion, green pepper and chilli in a large microwave-safe container and cook on HIGH (100%) for 2 minutes. Add rice and cook on HIGH (100%) for 1 minute longer. Mix in tomatoes, stock or water and cook, uncovered, on HIGH (100%) for 15-20 minutes or until liquid is absorbed and rice is tender. Season with black pepper.

1 tablespoon olive oil
1 onion, sliced
1 green pepper, sliced
1 red chilli, seeded and finely chopped
3/4 cup/170 g/5 1/2 oz white rice
3/4 cup/170 g/5 1/2 oz quick-cooking brown rice
440 g/14 oz canned tomatoes, undrained and mashed
1 1/2 cups/375 mL/12 fl oz vegetable stock or water
freshly ground black pepper

1 Heat oil in a large saucepan, add onion, green pepper and chilli and cook, stirring, for 5 minutes or until onion is soft. Add rice, mix well and cook for 3-4 minutes longer.

2 Add tomatoes and stock or water to pan and bring to the boil. Reduce heat and simmer for 30 minutes or until liquid is absorbed and rice is tender. Season to taste with black pepper

Serves 4

Marinated Tofu Salad

4 tablespoons soy sauce
2 teaspoons vegetable oil
1/2 teaspoon finely chopped fresh ginger
1 tablespoon lemon juice
2 teaspoons dry white wine
500 g/1 lb tofu, cut into cubes
1 lettuce, leaves separated
2 tomatoes, cut into wedges
60 g/2 oz snow pea sprouts
or watercress
2 carrots, sliced
1 tablespoon sesame seeds, toasted

1 Place soy sauce, oil, ginger, lemon juice and wine in a small bowl. Add tofu and toss to coat. Cover and set aside to marinate for 10-15 minutes.

2 Place lettuce, tomatoes, snow pea sprouts or watercress and carrots in a bowl. Drain tofu and reserve marinade. Add tofu to salad, toss to combine and sprinkle with sesame seeds. Just prior to serving, drizzle with reserved marinade.

Serves 4

An easy summer meal, this salad requires only wholegrain or rye bread to make it a complete meal.

Summer Frittata

30 g/1 oz butter
1 clove garlic, crushed
4 zucchini (courgettes), sliced
8 eggs, lightly beaten
2 tablespoons chopped sun-dried tomatoes
6 spring onions, finely chopped
1 tablespoon chopped fresh basil
1 tablespoon chopped fresh mint
freshly ground black pepper
30 g/1 oz grated tasty cheese (mature Cheddar)

1 Melt butter in a frying pan, add garlic and zucchini (courgettes) and cook over a medium heat for 5-6 minutes or until zucchini (courgettes) are just tender.

2 Place eggs, sun-dried tomatoes, spring onions, basil, mint and black pepper to taste in a bowl and mix to combine. Pour egg mixture over zucchini (courgette) mixture in pan and gently move vegetables to allow egg mixture to run under them. Reduce heat to low and cook until frittata is brown on the base and just set.

3 Sprinkle frittata with cheese and cook under a preheated medium grill for 4-5 minutes or until cheese melts.

Serves 6

To serve, cut the frittata into wedges. It is delicious hot, warm or at room temperature. Frittata served at room temperature makes a great picnic dish.

Tofu and Vegetable Strudel

Oven temperature 180°C, 350°F, Gas 4

12 sheets filo pastry
45 g/1½ oz butter, melted
2 teaspoons grated Parmesan cheese
2 teaspoons sesame seeds

VEGETABLE FILLING

200 g/6½ oz asparagus, chopped
2 carrots, grated
2 potatoes, grated
3 tablespoons tomato paste (purée)
350 g/11 oz tofu, cut into 1 cm/½ in cubes
3 tablespoons chopped fresh basil
100 g/3½ oz grated tasty cheese (mature Cheddar)
3 tablespoons sour cream
freshly ground black pepper

1 To make filling, boil, steam or microwave asparagus, carrots and potatoes, separately, until just tender. Drain. Place cooked vegetables, tomato paste (purée), tofu, basil, cheese, sour cream and black pepper to taste in a bowl and mix well to combine.

2 Layer 6 sheets of pastry, brushing each sheet with melted butter. Spoon half the filling along one long edge of pastry, leaving a 7.5 cm/3 in border, fold in edges and roll up carefully like a Swiss roll. Repeat with remaining pastry and filling to make a second strudel.

3 Carefully lift strudels onto a lightly oiled baking tray. Brush top with any remaining butter, sprinkle with Parmesan cheese and sesame seeds and bake for 25 minutes or until golden.

Serves 6

In this recipe you can replace the tofu with cream or cottage cheese if you wish. Well-drained canned asparagus can be used in place of fresh asparagus. If using canned asparagus there is no need to cook it.

Summer Frittata,
Tofu and Vegetable Strudel

Vegetable Burgers

vegetable oil
10 lettuce leaves
10 wholemeal rolls, split and toasted

MIXED VEGETABLE PATTIES
500 g/1 lb broccoli, chopped
500 g/1 lb zucchini (courgettes), chopped
250 g/8 oz carrots, chopped
2 onions, finely chopped
2 cloves garlic, crushed
3 tablespoons chopped fresh parsley
3 cups/185 g/6 oz breadcrumbs, made from stale bread
1/2 cup/60 g/2 oz flour, sifted
freshly ground black pepper

SPICY TOMATO SAUCE
1 tablespoon olive oil
1 onion, finely chopped
1 clove garlic, crushed
1 fresh red chilli, seeded and finely chopped
1 green pepper, finely chopped
440 g/14 oz canned tomatoes, undrained and mashed

1 To make patties, boil, steam or microwave broccoli, zucchini (courgettes) and carrots, separately, until tender. Drain, rinse under cold running water and pat dry with absorbent kitchen paper.

2 Place broccoli, zucchini (courgettes), carrots, onions, garlic and parsley in a food processor and process until puréed. Transfer vegetable mixture to a bowl, add breadcrumbs, flour and black pepper to taste and mix to combine. Cover and refrigerate for 30 minutes.

3 Shape mixture into 10 patties. Place on a tray lined with nonstick baking paper, cover and refrigerate until required.

4 To make sauce, heat olive oil in a saucepan, add onion, garlic, chilli and green pepper and cook for 5 minutes or until onion and green pepper are soft. Add tomatoes, bring to the boil, then reduce heat and simmer, stirring occasionally, for 15-20 minutes or until sauce reduces and thickens. Season to taste with black pepper.

5 Heat vegetable oil in a large frying pan, add patties and cook for 3-4 minutes each side or until browned and heated through. Place a lettuce leaf, a pattie, and a spoonful of sauce on the bottom half of each roll, top with remaining roll half and serve immediately.

Makes 10

These patties can also be cooked on a lightly oiled preheated barbecue plate (griddle) making them an ideal alternative to meat patties for vegetarians. You might be surprised at how many meat lovers want to eat them too, so make plenty.

Vegetable Burgers

Stuffed Peppers

3 red or green peppers
2 tablespoons wheat germ
30 g/1 oz grated tasty cheese (mature Cheddar)

VEGETABLE FILLING
1 cup/60 g/2 oz wholemeal breadcrumbs, made from stale bread
4 spring onions, chopped
1 large carrot, grated
2 zucchini (courgettes), grated
2 stalks celery, finely chopped
2 cloves garlic, crushed
60 g/2 oz hazelnuts, chopped
1/2 cup/100 g/3 1/2 oz natural yogurt

1 Cut peppers in half lengthwise and remove cores and seeds. Place pepper shells on a lightly oiled baking tray.

2 To make filling, place breadcrumbs, spring onions, carrot, zucchini (courgettes), celery, garlic, hazelnuts and yogurt in a bowl and mix to combine.

3 Divide filling between pepper shells and bake for 30 minutes. Combine wheat germ and cheese, sprinkle over filling and bake for 15 minutes longer or until cheese melts.

Serves 6

Oven temperature
180°C, 350°F, Gas 4

This filling can also be used to fill other vegetables such as zucchini (courgettes), pumpkin or eggplant (aubergine).

Sweet Potato Pie

Oven temperature
180°C, 350°F, Gas 4

This pie is delicious served hot, warm or cold. Cold it makes an ideal picnic dish.

1/2 cup/100 g/3 1/2 oz brown rice, cooked
1 egg, lightly beaten

SWEET POTATO FILLING
500 g/1 lb sweet potato, chopped
2 teaspoons curry powder
15 g/1/2 oz butter
1 teaspoon garam masala
1/2 teaspoon ground coriander
1/2 teaspoon ground cumin
250 g/8 oz mushrooms, chopped
1 small red pepper, finely chopped
4 spring onions, chopped
2 cloves garlic, crushed
1 egg, lightly beaten with
1 tablespoon milk

1 Place rice and egg in a bowl and mix to combine. Press rice mixture into the base and up the sides of a lightly greased 23 cm/9 in pie plate.

2 To make filling, boil, steam or microwave sweet potato until tender. Drain and mash with curry powder. Set aside to cool. Melt butter in a saucepan, add garam masala, coriander, cumin, mushrooms, red pepper, spring onions and garlic and cook, stirring frequently, for 10 minutes or until almost all the liquid has evaporated. Remove pan from heat and set aside to cool. Add mushroom mixture and egg mixture to mashed sweet potato and mix to combine. Spoon filling into pie plate and bake for 25 minutes or until filling is set.

Serves 4

Vegetable Kebabs

2 zucchini (courgettes), cut into 1 cm/1/2 in pieces
16 button mushrooms
1 red pepper, cut into 2.5 cm/1 in squares
4 canned pineapple slices, drained and each cut into 8 pieces

BASIL GLAZE
3 tablespoons olive oil
1 tablespoon balsamic vinegar
1 teaspoon chopped fresh basil
1 clove garlic, crushed
1 teaspoon grated lime or lemon rind
freshly ground black pepper

NUTTY AVOCADO SAUCE
1 small ripe avocado, stoned, peeled and roughly chopped
3 tablespoons natural yogurt
1 tablespoon lemon juice
2 tablespoons finely chopped walnuts
2 teaspoons cider vinegar
pinch cayenne pepper

1 Thread zucchini (courgettes), mushrooms, red pepper and pineapple pieces, alternately, onto eight oiled wooden skewers.

2 To make glaze, place oil, vinegar, basil, garlic, lime or lemon rind and black pepper to taste in a bowl and whisk to combine. Brush glaze over kebabs and grill or barbecue, brushing with glaze and turning frequently, for 8-10 minutes or until vegetables are tender.

3 To make sauce, place avocado, yogurt, lemon juice, walnuts, vinegar and cayenne pepper in a food processor or blender and process until smooth. Serve with kebabs.

Serves 4

Sweet Potato Pie,
Vegetable Kebabs

Spinach and Rice Balls

1 bunch/500 g/1 lb spinach, leaves finely chopped
1/2 cup/100 g/3 1/2 oz rice, cooked
1/2 teaspoon ground nutmeg
2 tablespoons grated Parmesan cheese
2 tablespoons grated lemon rind
125 g/4 oz grated tasty cheese (mature Cheddar)
3 eggs
freshly ground black pepper
2 cups/125 g/4 oz breadcrumbs, made from stale bread
vegetable oil for deep-frying

TOMATO SAUCE
15 g/1/2 oz butter
1 onion, chopped
440 g/14 oz canned tomatoes, undrained and mashed
2 tablespoons chopped fresh basil

For something different, you might like to make these rice balls using brown rice or a combination of white and brown rice. This is also a good way to use up any leftover rice you might have.

1 Steam or microwave spinach until wilted, drain, squeeze out excess liquid and place in a bowl. Add rice, nutmeg, Parmesan cheese, lemon rind, cheese, 2 eggs and black pepper to taste and mix to combine.

2 Roll heaped teaspoons of rice mixture into balls and set aside. Place remaining egg in a small bowl and whisk. Dip rice balls in egg, then roll in breadcrumbs and place on a plate lined with plastic food wrap, cover and refrigerate for 30 minutes.

3 To make sauce, melt butter in a saucepan, add onion and cook, stirring, for 4-5 minutes or until onion is soft. Add tomatoes, bring to the boil, then reduce heat and simmer, stirring occasionally, for 10-15 minutes or until sauce thickens and reduces. Stir in basil.

4 Heat oil in a deep saucepan until a cube of bread dropped in browns in 50 seconds. Cook 3-4 rice balls at a time for 4-5 minutes until golden and heated through. Drain on absorbent kitchen paper and serve with Tomato Sauce.

Makes 16

Cauliflower Croquettes

Oven temperature
180°C, 350°F, Gas 4

1 cauliflower, broken into florets
2 eggs, lightly beaten
1/2 cup/15 g/1/2 oz unprocessed bran
4 tablespoons ricotta cheese
2 tablespoons chopped fresh parsley
3 tablespoons snipped fresh chives
60 g/2 oz grated tasty cheese (mature Cheddar)

1 Boil, steam or microwave cauliflower until very tender. Drain well and place in a bowl.

2 Mash cauliflower, then add eggs, bran, ricotta cheese, parsley and chives and mix to combine.

3 Shape cauliflower mixture into croquettes and place in a lightly greased ovenproof dish. Sprinkle with cheese and bake for 20 minutes.

Serves 4

Carrot Balls

3 carrots, grated
2 teaspoons orange rind
60 g/2 oz grated Swiss cheese
60 g/2 oz grated Parmesan cheese
1 tablespoon chopped fresh mint
freshly ground black pepper
2 eggs, lightly beaten
1 cup/30 g/1 oz unprocessed bran
3 tablespoons finely chopped almonds
flour
vegetable oil for deep-frying

1 Place carrots, orange rind, Swiss cheese, Parmesan cheese, mint, black pepper to taste and half the egg mixture in a bowl and mix to combine. Shape carrot mixture into balls.

2 Place bran and almonds in a bowl and mix to combine. Roll balls in flour, then dip in remaining egg mixture and roll in bran mixture. Place balls on a plate lined with plastic food wrap and refrigerate for 30 minutes.

3 Heat oil in a large saucepan until a cube of bread dropped in browns in 50 seconds. Cook balls a few at a time for 4-5 minutes or until golden and heated through. Drain on absorbent kitchen paper and serve immediately.

Serves 4

Carrot Balls

QUICK MEALS

As most vegetables take only minutes to cook, they lend themselves to quick-cooking techniques. Next time you need to make a meal in a hurry, why not try the filling Beans Con Carne or Puff Mushroom Pizza.

Vegetable Vol-au-Vents

Vegetable Vol-au-Vents

30 g/1 oz butter
1 onion, chopped
2 cloves garlic, crushed
375 g/12 oz zucchini (courgettes), sliced
185 g/6 oz mushrooms, sliced
2 tablespoons flour
1½ cups/375 mL/12 fl oz milk
60 g/2 oz grated tasty cheese (mature Cheddar)
1 tablespoon tomato paste (purée)
2 tablespoons chopped fresh parsley
½ teaspoon dried oregano
freshly ground black pepper
6 x 10 cm/4 in vol-au-vent pastry cases

1 Melt butter in a saucepan, add onion and garlic and cook over a medium heat, stirring frequently, until onion is tender. Add zucchini (courgettes) and mushrooms and cook, stirring occasionally, for 4-5 minutes longer or until vegetables are tender.

2 Stir in flour and cook for 1 minute. Gradually stir in milk and bring to the boil. Reduce heat and simmer, stirring constantly, for 3 minutes or until mixture thickens. Remove pan from heat and stir in cheese, tomato paste (purée), parsley, oregano and black pepper to taste.

3 Heat vol-au-vent cases in the oven for 10 minutes. Spoon hot vegetable mixture into vol-au-vent cases and serve immediately.

Serves 6

Oven temperature
180°C, 350°F, Gas 4

To ensure crisp and flaky pastry, always reheat and fill vol-au-vent cases just prior to serving.

Potato Pancake

1 large potato, grated
2 tablespoons flour
1 egg, lightly beaten
1 tablespoon grated Parmesan cheese
1 tablespoon snipped fresh chives
freshly ground black pepper
2 teaspoons vegetable oil

1 Squeeze as much moisture as possible from potato. Place potato, flour, egg, Parmesan cheese, chives and black pepper to taste in a bowl and mix to combine.

2 Heat oil in a small frying pan. Spoon potato mixture into pan, spread over base and cook for 4-5 minutes each side or until golden.

Serves 1

Serve pancake topped with sour cream, tasty cheese (mature Cheddar) and freshly ground black pepper; chopped chicken and avocado; or pan-cooked onion, tomato, mushrooms and chopped fresh parsley or chives.

Beans Con Carne

3 tablespoons water
2 onions, chopped
2 cloves garlic, crushed
1 red pepper, chopped
2 x 440 g/14 oz canned red kidney beans, drained
2 carrots, diced
250 g/8 oz green beans, cut into 2.5 cm/1 in pieces
2 x 440 g/14 oz canned tomatoes, undrained and mashed
1 cup/250 mL/8 fl oz tomato juice
1/4 teaspoon chilli powder, or according to taste
4 tablespoons chopped fresh parsley

1 Heat water in a saucepan, add onion and garlic and cook, stirring, for 3-4 minutes or until onion is soft.

2 Add red pepper, red kidney beans, carrots, green beans, tomatoes, tomato juice and chilli powder and bring to the boil. Reduce heat and simmer, stirring occasionally, for 15-20 minutes or until mixture reduces and thickens. Stir in parsley and serve.

***Serves* 6**

For a complete meal, accompany with rice, pasta or crusty bread and a tossed green salad.

Peppers filled with Beans

Oven temperature 180°C, 350°F, Gas 4

4 red or green peppers

BEAN FILLING
2 tablespoons olive oil
1 onion, chopped
2 tablespoons ground cumin
1 clove garlic, crushed
3 tablespoons tomato paste (purée)
1/4 cup/60 mL/2 fl oz chicken or vegetable stock
440 g/14 oz canned tomatoes, undrained and mashed
440 g/14 oz canned red kidney beans, drained
freshly ground black pepper

1 Cut peppers in half lengthwise and remove seeds and pith. Place pepper shells on a lightly greased baking tray and set aside.

2 Heat oil in a large saucepan, add onion and cook, stirring, for 2-3 minutes or until onion is soft.

3 Add cumin, garlic, tomato paste (purée), stock, tomatoes and red kidney beans to pan and bring to the boil. Reduce heat and simmer, uncovered, for 10 minutes or until mixture reduces and thickens. Season to taste with black pepper.

4 Spoon filling into prepared pepper shells and bake for 20 minutes or until peppers are tender.

***Serves* 4**

This tasty combination of red kidney beans and tomatoes is also delicious served on its own, or you might like to try it as a filling for baby pumpkins.

Beans Con Carne,
Peppers filled with Beans

Right: Puff Mushroom Pizza
Below: Broad Beans and Ham

Broad Beans and Ham

500 g/1 lb shelled or frozen broad beans
1 tablespoon vegetable oil
185 g/6 oz ham, cut into thin strips
1 tablespoon flour
1/4 cup/60 mL/2 fl oz dry white wine
3/4 cup/185 mL/6 fl oz chicken or vegetable stock
1 tablespoon cream (double)
freshly ground black pepper
1 tablespoon chopped mixed fresh herbs

1 Boil, steam or microwave broad beans until tender. Drain and set aside.

2 Heat oil in a large frying pan, add ham and cook over a medium heat for 1 minute. Stir in flour and cook for 1 minute longer.

3 Stir wine, stock, cream and black pepper to taste into pan and bring to the boil, stirring constantly. Reduce heat and simmer for 5 minutes or until sauce thickens. Add broad beans and herbs and cook for 1 minute longer.

Serves 4

This recipe is a great way to use up leftover ham and is just as delicious made with diced cold beef or lamb, chicken or turkey.

Puff Mushroom Pizza

375 g/12 oz prepared puff pastry
60 g/2 oz grated Parmesan cheese
125 g/4 oz grated mozzarella cheese
1 onion, thinly sliced
200 g/6 1/2 oz mushrooms, sliced
3 tomatoes, cut into 1 cm/1/2 in slices
10 pitted black olives
2 teaspoons chopped fresh oregano or 1/2 teaspoon dried oregano
2 teaspoons chopped fresh thyme or 1/2 teaspoon dried thyme

1 Roll out pastry to fit a greased 26 x 32 cm/10 1/2 x 12 3/4 in Swiss roll tin.

2 Sprinkle pastry with Parmesan cheese and mozzarella cheese, then top with onion, mushrooms, tomatoes and olives. Sprinkle with oregano and thyme and bake for 30 minutes or until pastry is puffed and golden. Serve hot, warm or cold.

Serves 6

Oven temperature
200°C, 400°F, Gas 6

This quick pastry-based pizza is great for weekend meals and leftovers are ideal for packed lunches.

Spinach and Bacon Salad

1 tablespoon olive oil
4 rashers bacon, chopped
90 g/3 oz slivered almonds
1 bunch/500 g/1 lb spinach, roughly chopped

BLUE CHEESE DRESSING
60 g/2 oz blue vein cheese, crumbled
1 tablespoon mayonnaise
1 tablespoon sour cream
$^1/_4$ cup/60 mL/2 fl oz cream (double)

1 Heat oil in a large frying pan, add bacon and cook over a medium heat for 3-4 minutes or until bacon is crispy. Add almonds and cook, stirring, for 3 minutes longer or until almonds are golden.

2 Arrange spinach on a large serving platter, top with bacon, almonds and any pan juices and toss to combine.

3 To make dressing, place cheese, mayonnaise, sour cream and cream in a bowl and mix to combine. Drizzle dressing over salad and serve immediately.

Serves 4

The hot bacon mixture will wilt the spinach leaves slightly. The secret to making warm salads such as this one is to make and serve them immediately. For a complete meal, serve with crusty bread or rolls.

Left: Vegetable Omelette
Far left: Spinach and Bacon Salad

VEGETABLE OMELETTE

90 g/3 oz butter
1 leek, sliced
375 g/12 oz finely chopped mixed vegetables of your choice
1 clove garlic, crushed
1 teaspoon mustard seeds
6 eggs
3 tablespoons water
freshly ground black pepper

1 Melt 60 g/2 oz butter in a frying pan, add leek, mixed vegetables, garlic and mustard seeds and cook over a medium heat, stirring, for 5 minutes or until vegetables are tender. Remove vegetables from pan, set aside and keep warm.

2 Place eggs, water and black pepper to taste in a bowl and whisk to combine. Melt 15 g/$^1/_2$ oz butter in pan, pour in half the egg mixture and cook over a medium heat. Continually draw in edge of omelette with a fork during cooking until no liquid remains and omelette is lightly set. Spoon half the vegetable mixture onto omelette and fold over. Repeat with remaining butter, egg mixture and vegetable mixture to make a second omelette.

Serves 2

Using some of the frozen mixed-vegetable varieties for this recipe cuts down on preparation time, as the chopping of the vegetables is eliminated. The cooking time will remain the same.

SIDE DISHES

Vegetables feature as accompaniments to nearly every main meal. An interesting vegetable dish can turn a plain grilled steak into a meal to remember. The simple vegetable dishes in this collection are sure to inspire you.

Broad Beans with Yogurt, Honeyed Onions

Broad Beans with Yogurt

2 tablespoons olive oil
1 kg/2 lb shelled or frozen broad beans
2 tablespoons snipped fresh chives
1/4 cup/60 mL/2 fl oz lemon juice
2 tablespoons chopped fresh dill
2 cups/500 mL/16 fl oz water
3/4 cup/185 g/6 oz natural yogurt
2 cloves garlic, crushed

1 Heat oil in a large saucepan, add broad beans and chives and cook, stirring constantly, for 3 minutes.

2 Stir in lemon juice, dill and water and bring to the boil. Reduce heat and simmer for 10 minutes. Drain beans, transfer to a serving dish and set aside to cool.

3 Place yogurt and garlic in a small bowl and mix to combine. Spoon yogurt mixture over beans and serve immediately or chill.

Serves 6

Serve this tasty broad bean dish hot or chilled depending on the occasion and the weather.

Honeyed Onions

20 baby white onions, halved lengthwise
60 g/2 oz butter
2 tablespoons honey

1 Bring a large saucepan of water to the boil, add onions and cook for 5 minutes. Drain onions and set aside.

2 Melt butter and honey in a large frying pan. Add onions and cook over a medium heat, turning frequently, for 5-10 minutes or until onions are golden.

Serves 6

Onions that are to be used whole should be peeled carefully so that the firm base holding the onion together is left intact. This ensures that the onions do not fall apart during cooking.

'The onion has been cultivated for food since very early times and can be traced to ancient Egypt.'

Roast Potatoes with Bacon

Oven temperature
180°C, 350°F, Gas 4

4 large potatoes, quartered
1/4 cup/60 mL/2 fl oz vegetable oil
1 tablespoon hazelnut or walnut oil
6 rashers bacon, chopped
1/4 teaspoon ground nutmeg
freshly ground black pepper

1 Bring a large saucepan of water to the boil, add potatoes and cook for 5 minutes. Drain potatoes and pat dry with absorbent kitchen paper.

2 Place potatoes in a baking dish. Combine vegetable and hazelnut or walnut oils, pour over potatoes and toss to coat.

3 Bake potatoes for 30 minutes, turning occasionally. Sprinkle with bacon and nutmeg and season to taste with black pepper. Bake for 10 minutes longer or until potatoes are tender and bacon is cooked and crisp.

Serves 6

If hazelnut or walnut oil is unavailable you can use olive or vegetable oil for this recipe.

Ricotta-filled Potatoes

Oven temperature
180°C, 350°F, Gas 4

4 large potatoes
1/2 cup/125 g/8 oz ricotta cheese
2 tablespoons grated Parmesan cheese
4 canned asparagus spears, drained and chopped
1 tablespoon snipped fresh chives
freshly ground black pepper
2 tablespoons chopped hazelnuts or walnuts

1 Boil or microwave potatoes until tender. Drain and set aside until cool enough to handle. Cut tops from potatoes and scoop out flesh leaving a 5 mm/1/4 in shell.

2 Place potato flesh, ricotta cheese, Parmesan cheese, asparagus, chives and black pepper to taste in a bowl and mix to combine.

3 Spoon potato mixture into potato shells, sprinkle with hazelnuts or walnuts and bake for 20-25 minutes or until heated through.

Serves 4

Did you know? When first introduced to Europe from South America, potatoes were thought to have weakening properties, or even to be a cause of leprosy. Today they are recognised as an important source of complex carbohydrate, fibre, protein, vitamins and minerals.

Roast Potatoes with Bacon,
Ricotta-filled Potatoes

Sweet Potato Crisps

500 g/1 lb sweet potatoes
2 tablespoons lemon juice
vegetable oil for deep-frying
1 tablespoon salt
1 teaspoon chilli powder, or according to taste
$^{1}/_{2}$ teaspoon caster sugar

There are several varieties of sweet potato: the two most common are the white and the orange sweet potato. The white variety has a creamy yellow flesh and a dry mealy texture while the orange variety has a yellow- to deep orange-coloured flesh and a sweet, almost chestnut-like, flavour.

1 Slice potatoes into paper thin slices. Place potato slices and lemon juice in a large bowl, cover with cold water and refrigerate for 2 hours. Drain and pat dry with absorbent kitchen paper.

2 Heat oil in a large saucepan until a cube of bread dropped in browns in 50 seconds. Add potato slices a few at a time and cook for 5-6 minutes or until potatoes are golden and almost crisp. Remove crisps from oil and drain on absorbent kitchen paper.

3 Just prior to serving, return cooked potatoes to hot oil and cook until crisp. Remove from oil and drain on absorbent kitchen paper.

4 Combine salt, chilli powder and sugar, sprinkle over hot crisps and toss to coat. Serve immediately.

Serves 4

Potato and Carrot Nest

Oven temperature
180°C, 350°F, Gas 4

4 large potatoes
2 egg yolks
$^{1}/_{4}$ teaspoon ground nutmeg
60 g/2 oz butter
freshly ground black pepper

CARROT PUREE
6 large carrots
$^{3}/_{4}$ cup/185 mL/6 fl oz chicken stock
2 tablespoons orange juice
$^{1}/_{4}$ teaspoon ground nutmeg

For something different try using sweet potatoes in place of the potatoes in this recipe and accompany them with parsnip purée, using lemon juice in place of the orange juice.

1 Boil or microwave potatoes until tender. Drain, place in a bowl and mash. Add egg yolks, nutmeg, half the butter and black pepper to taste and mix well to combine.

2 Spoon potato mixture into a piping bag fitted with a large star nozzle and pipe a decorative border around the outer edge of an ovenproof dish. Spoon any remaining potato into centre of dish and spread out over base. Brush with remaining butter and bake for 20 minutes or until golden.

3 To make purée, place carrots and stock in a saucepan and bring to the boil. Reduce heat, cover and simmer for 10-15 minutes or until carrots are tender. Set aside to cool for 10 minutes then transfer carrots and stock to a food processor or blender and process until smooth. Return carrot purée to pan, add orange juice and nutmeg and cook over a low heat, stirring, for 4-5 minutes or until heated through. Spoon purée into centre of potato nest and serve immediately.

Serves 6

Pear and Spinach Salad

1 bunch/500 g/1 lb spinach, stalks removed and leaves shredded
2 spring onions, chopped
3 slices ham, cut into thin strips
2 pears, peeled, cored and diced

MUSTARD DRESSING
2 tablespoons lemon juice
1 tablespoon wholegrain mustard
2 teaspoons sugar
1 teaspoon dried tarragon
2 tablespoons olive oil
1/2 cup/125 mL/4 fl oz vegetable oil
freshly ground black pepper

1 Place spinach, spring onions, ham and pears in a large serving dish.

2 To make dressing, place lemon juice, mustard, sugar, tarragon, olive oil, vegetable oil and black pepper to taste in a screwtop jar and shake well to combine. Spoon dressing over salad and toss to combine.

Serves 6

Apples or nashi pears could be used in this salad in place of the pears if you wish.

Potato and Carrot Nest, Pear and Spinach Salad

Potatoes with Red Pepper

Oven temperature
180°C, 350°F, Gas 4

Vegetarians can omit the bacon from this recipe.

3 large potatoes, cut into 5 mm/^{1}/4 in slices
2 onions, chopped
2 red peppers, cut into thin strips
2 rashers bacon, cut into thin strips
1 tablespoon chopped fresh sage
^{1}/4 cup/60 mL/2 fl oz olive oil
freshly ground black pepper

1 Layer potatoes, onions, red peppers and bacon in a large baking dish.

2 Place sage, oil and black pepper to taste in a small bowl and mix to combine. Pour over vegetable mixture and bake, turning occasionally, for 40 minutes or until potatoes are tender.

Serves 6

Peas with Prosciutto

Peas are rich in protein, fibre and B-group vitamins.

3 tablespoons olive oil
30 g/1 oz butter
1 onion, chopped
6 slices prosciutto or bacon, cut into strips
500 g/1 lb shelled or frozen peas
1 cup/250 mL/8 fl oz water
1 tablespoon chopped fresh parsley
freshly ground black pepper

1 Heat oil and butter in a large frying pan, add onion and prosciutto or bacon and cook, stirring, for 3 minutes.

2 Add peas and water to pan, bring to the boil, reduce heat and simmer for 10-15 minutes or until peas are cooked.

3 Strain peas and place in a serving dish. Add parsley and black pepper to taste and toss to combine. Serve immediately.

Serves 4

'Green peas are thought to have originated in the eastern Mediterranean areas. In Iran and Afghanistan wild forms are still found.'

Potatoes with Red Pepper,
Peas with Proscuitto

Right: Potato Croquettes
Far right: Brussels Sprouts and Almonds

Potato Croquettes

500 g/1 lb potatoes, cut into quarters
100 g/3$^{1}/_{2}$ oz wholemeal breadcrumbs
4 spring onions, chopped
250 g/8 oz cottage cheese
1 egg, lightly beaten
1 tablespoon chopped fresh parsley
1 tablespoon chopped fresh oregano or 1 teaspoon dried oregano
freshly ground black pepper
1$^{1}/_{2}$ cups/230 g/7$^{1}/_{2}$ oz wholemeal flour
vegetable oil for deep-frying

1 Place potatoes in a saucepan of water and bring to the boil. Reduce heat, cover and simmer for 20-25 minutes or until potatoes are cooked. Drain potatoes and press through a sieve into a bowl.

2 Add breadcrumbs, spring onions, cottage cheese, egg, parsley, oregano and black pepper to taste to potatoes and mix to combine. Cover and refrigerate until potato mixture is cold.

3 Divide potato mixture into 12 portions and shape into croquettes. Roll each croquette in flour and place on a plate lined with plastic food wrap.

4 Heat oil in a large saucepan until a cube of bread dropped in browns in 50 seconds. Cook a few croquettes at a time for 4-5 minutes or until golden and heated through. Drain on absorbent kitchen paper and serve immediately.

Serves 4

Potato Croquettes make an interesting alternative to potatoes when served as an accompaniment to a meal, or are delicious as a light meal served with salad and mango chutney.

Brussels Sprouts and Almonds

500 g/1 lb Brussels sprouts
3 tablespoons toasted flaked almonds

MUSTARD SAUCE
30 g/1 oz butter
2 tablespoons brown sugar
3 teaspoons cornflour
1/2 teaspoon prepared hot English mustard
1 small onion, finely chopped
3 tablespoons white vinegar

1 Boil, steam or microwave Brussels sprouts until tender. Drain, set aside and keep warm.

2 To make sauce, melt butter in a small saucepan, stir in brown sugar, cornflour, mustard, onion and vinegar and cook over a medium heat, stirring, for 2-3 minutes or until sauce boils and thickens. Pour sauce over Brussels sprouts and toss to coat. Sprinkle with almonds and serve immediately.

Serves 4

This is an easy and tasty way to serve Brussels sprouts. Broccoli is also delicious cooked this way.

Daikon and Carrot Salad

1 daikon, cut into thin strips
1 large carrot, cut into thin strips
2 teaspoons salt

CHILLI DRESSING
1/2 cup/125 mL/4 fl oz rice vinegar
1 small red chilli, finely chopped
2 tablespoons brown sugar
1 tablespoon lemon juice

1 Place daikon and carrot in a colander set over a bowl, sprinkle with salt and set aside to stand for 10 minutes. Rinse daikon and carrot under cold running water, drain, pat dry with absorbent kitchen paper and place in a bowl.

2 To make dressing, place vinegar, chilli, brown sugar and lemon juice in a screwtop jar and shake well to combine. Spoon dressing over vegetable mixture and toss to combine. Cover and set aside to stand for 1 hour before serving.

Serves 6

Daikon is the Japanese, or giant, white radish. A typical one may have a diameter of 5 cm/2 in and a length of 25 cm/10 in. It has a hot peppery taste. If daikon is unavailable, you can use radishes instead.

Chinese Broccoli Stir-Fry

1 bunch Chinese broccoli
1 tablespoon vegetable oil
1 clove garlic, crushed
1 tablespoon finely chopped fresh ginger
1/2 cup/125 mL/4 fl oz chicken or vegetable stock blended with 2 teaspoons cornflour
1 teaspoon soy sauce
1 teaspoon sesame oil

1 Separate broccoli leaves from stems. Set leaves and any flowers aside. Peel stems and cut into 5 cm/2 in strips. Cook stems in boiling water for 3-4 minutes or until just tender. Drain, refresh under cold running water, drain again and set aside.

2 Heat oil in a wok or large frying pan, add garlic, ginger and broccoli stems and stir-fry for 1-2 minutes. Add broccoli leaves and flowers and stir-fry for 3-4 minutes longer or until leaves are soft.

3 Add stock mixture, soy sauce and sesame oil to pan and stir for 1-2 minutes or until sauce boils and thickens. Serve immediately.

Serves 4

Chinese broccoli has a stem similar to ordinary broccoli, but bears no other resemblance to it. The easiest way to prepare it is to trim the base of each stem and peel it with a vegetable peeler. Slice the stems and blanch for a few minutes in boiling water to tenderise.

Daikon and Carrot Salad,
Chinese Broccoli Stir-Fry

Carrot Gnocchi with Vegetable Sauce

CARROT GNOCCHI
30 g/1 oz butter
1 onion, chopped
2 cloves garlic, crushed
500 g/1 lb carrots, finely grated
250 g/8 oz ricotta cheese
125 g/4 oz grated Parmesan cheese
1 cup/125 g/4 oz flour
1 egg yolk, lightly beaten
ground nutmeg
freshly ground black pepper
60 g/2 oz butter, melted

VEGETABLE SAUCE
2 tablespoons olive oil
3 large zucchini (courgettes), sliced
6 spring onions, chopped
3/4 cup/185 mL/6 fl oz cream (double)

1 To make gnocchi, melt butter in a small saucepan, add onion and garlic and cook for 4-5 minutes or until onion is soft. Transfer onion mixture to a large bowl, add carrots, ricotta cheese, 60 g/2 oz Parmesan cheese, 2 tablespoons flour, egg yolk, 1/4 teaspoon nutmeg and black pepper to taste and mix well to combine.

2 Form small spoonfuls of mixture into egg shapes and toss in remaining flour. Shake off excess flour from gnocchi, place on a plate lined with plastic food wrap and refrigerate for 30 minutes or until gnocchi are firm.

3 Bring a large saucepan of water to the boil and cook gnocchi a few at a time for 3-5 minutes or until they rise to the surface. Using a slotted spoon, remove gnocchi from pan, set aside and keep warm.

4 To make sauce, heat oil in a saucepan, add zucchini (courgettes) and spring onions and cook, stirring, for 4-5 minutes or until vegetables are soft. Remove pan from heat and set aside to cool slightly. Transfer vegetable mixture to a food processor or blender and process until smooth. Return vegetable purée to a clean saucepan, stir in cream and season to taste with black pepper. Cook sauce over a low heat, stirring, until almost boiling.

For a complete meal, serve gnocchi with a tossed green salad or steamed vegetables and crusty bread or rolls.

5 To serve, spoon sauce into a serving dish, top with gnocchi, pour over melted butter, sprinkle with remaining Parmesan cheese and dust with nutmeg.

Serves 6

Potato Baskets

To make these baskets, it is easier to use a special frying basket. If you do not have one, you can use 2 Chinese wire frying spoons instead.

Potato Baskets look great filled with steamed or stir-fried vegetables as an accompaniment to a meal. They also make the perfect container for deep-fried seafood.

2 large potatoes, thinly sliced
vegetable oil for deep-frying

1 Dip the frying basket in oil to prevent the Potato Baskets sticking during cooking. Arrange overlapping potato slices in frying basket, fold basket over potato slices and clip in position.

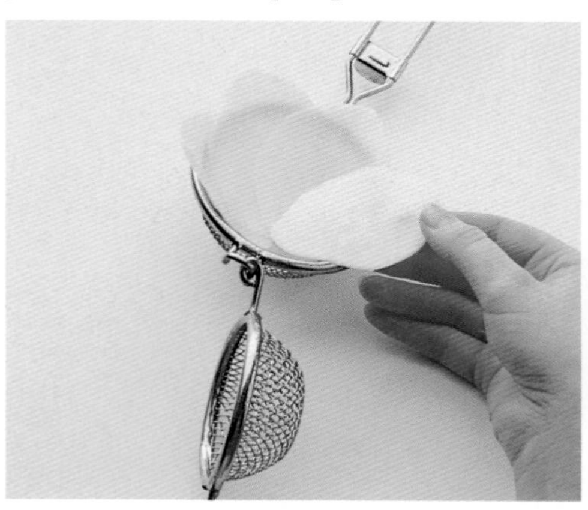

2 Heat oil in a large saucepan until a cube of bread dropped in browns in 50 seconds. Lower basket into hot oil and cook potato basket for 4-5 minutes or until golden. Remove basket from oil, drain and remove potato basket. Repeat with remaining potato slices.

3 Just prior to serving, reheat oil and cook Potato Baskets one at a time until golden. Drain and use as desired.

Makes 4 baskets

CREAMY POTATO SKINS

1.5 kg/3 lb potatoes
90 g/3 oz butter, melted
salt
1 cup/250 g/8 oz sour cream
2 tablespoons snipped fresh chives

Oven temperature
200°C, 400°F, Gas 4

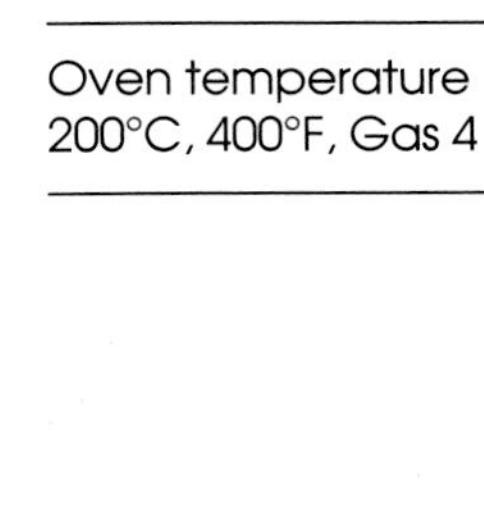

1 Scrub potatoes, pierce with a fork and bake for 1 hour or until potatoes are tender.

2 Cut potatoes into quarters and carefully remove flesh, leaving a 5 mm/ 1/4 in shell. Reserve the cooked potato for another use.

3 Increase oven temperature to 240°C/ 475°F/Gas 8. Brush both surfaces of potato skins with melted butter, place on a baking tray, sprinkle with salt and bake for 10-15 minutes or until skins are crisp.

4 Place sour cream and chives in a small bowl and mix to combine. Serve with potato skins.

Serves 6

Potato skins make a great snack or first course. You might like to try serving them with a yogurt and mint dip or an avocado dip.

Vegetable Samosas

These wonderful spicy pastry snacks can be found throughout Asia. Sometimes they contain a meat and vegetable filling. This recipe is ideal for vegetarians.

250 g/8 oz potatoes, chopped
2 tablespoons vegetable oil
1 onion, finely chopped
1/2 teaspoon cumin seeds
1 teaspoon grated fresh ginger
1/2 teaspoon ground turmeric
1/2 teaspoon garam masala
125 g/4 oz shelled or frozen peas, cooked
2 teaspoons lemon juice
vegetable oil for deep-frying

PASTRY

1 cup/125 g/4 oz flour
30 g/1 oz butter
2 tablespoons warm milk

1 Boil potatoes for 15-20 minutes or until tender. Drain well, return to saucepan and shake over a low heat to dry off. Transfer potatoes to a bowl and mash well.

2 Heat oil in a large frying pan, add onion, cumin seeds, ginger, turmeric and garam masala and cook, stirring, for 5 minutes.

3 Add onion mixture to mashed potatoes and mix to combine. Add peas and lemon juice, mix and set aside to cool.

4 To make pastry, sift flour into a bowl. Using fingertips, rub in butter until mixture resembles fine breadcrumbs. Add milk and mix to form a stiff dough. Alternatively, the pastry can be made in the food processor. Place flour and butter in food processor and process until mixture resembles fine breadcrumbs, then, with machine running, add milk to form a stiff dough.

5 Divide dough into six portions and roll each portion into a ball. On a lightly floured surface roll out each ball to form a 15 cm/6 in circle. Cut each circle in half and top with filling.

6 Brush edges of pastry with a little water, then fold pastry over filling to form triangular-shaped pastries and seal. Heat oil in a deep saucepan until a cube of bread dropped in browns in 50 seconds. Cook samosas a few at a time for 3-4 minutes or until puffed and golden. Drain on absorbent kitchen paper and serve immediately.

Makes 12

Samosas are delicious served with mango chutney as a starter or snack.

Spanish Omelette

1 tablespoon olive oil
15 g/$^{1}/_{2}$ oz butter
1 onion, chopped
1 clove garlic, crushed
1 red pepper, diced
90 g/3 oz cabbage, finely shredded
4 rashers bacon, chopped
1 teaspoon dried fenugreek
$^{1}/_{2}$ teaspoon ground coriander
4 eggs, beaten
1 tablespoon cold water
freshly ground black pepper
60 g/2 oz grated tasty cheese
(mature Cheddar)

1 Heat oil and butter together in a 20 cm/ 8 in frying pan, add onion, garlic, red pepper, cabbage and bacon and cook over a low heat, stirring, for 5 minutes. Add fenugreek and coriander and mix well.

2 Place eggs, water and black pepper to taste in a bowl and whisk to combine. Pour egg mixture into pan, swirling pan to ensure an even coating and cook over a low heat for 5-6 minutes or until omelette is golden on the base and almost set on the top. Sprinkle with cheese and cook under a preheated grill for 3-4 minutes or until cheese is melted and omelette is set. Cut into wedges and serve immediately.

Serves 4

For a complete meal, accompany with a tossed green salad and crusty bread or rolls.

Roast Pepper Relish

1 red pepper, halved and seeded
1 green pepper, halved and seeded
1 yellow pepper, halved and seeded
1 onion, thinly sliced
1/3 cup/90 mL/3 fl oz vegetable oil
2 tablespoons lemon juice
1 teaspoon wholegrain mustard
1 clove garlic, crushed
1/2 teaspoon garam masala
2 teaspoons caster sugar
freshly ground black pepper

1 Place red, green and yellow pepper halves on a baking tray and bake for 30 minutes or until skins blister and char. Remove peppers from oven, place in a paper bag and set aside until peppers are cool enough to handle.

2 Peel skins from peppers. Cut peppers into quarters then into thin strips. Place peppers and onions in a bowl and mix to combine.

3 Place oil, lemon juice, mustard, garlic, garam masala, sugar and black pepper to taste in a screwtop jar and shake well to combine. Pour oil mixture over peppers, mix to combine, cover and refrigerate for 2-3 hours or overnight. Serve chilled.

Serves 4

Oven temperature
200°C, 400°F, Gas 6

This relish is delicious served with cold meats, cheese and crusty bread.

Making the Most of Vegetables

Health authorities recommend that we eat at least four serves of vegetables daily. Most of the vitamin content lies just under the skin, so vegetables should be cooked and eaten with the skin on as often as possible. Remember to also include raw vegetables regularly as these have the highest vitamin and nutrient content of all.

Equipment

All that you need to successfully prepare vegetables is a sharp vegetable or paring knife and a large chopping board. However to make life easier for you, it is worth investing a little time and money in a few other pieces of good equipment, such as several larger sharp knives for cutting and chopping, a grater, a vegetable peeler and a colander or large sieve. Remember to keep your knives sharp and either learn to sharpen them yourself or take them to a knife sharpener regularly. Sharp knives make preparation a breeze.

Vegetable Preparation

❧ Wash vegetables before preparing, but do not soak. Soaking tends to draw out the valuable water-soluble vitamins thereby decreasing the nutrient content. As with every rule there are always exceptions and it may be necessary to soak very dirty vegetables to remove dirt and creepy-crawlies. If this is the case, always keep soaking times to a minimum.

❧ Vegetables that are left whole with their skins on have a higher nutrient and fibre content than those that are finely chopped and peeled. Many of the precious vitamins and minerals found in vegetables are stored just under the skin. Only peel vegetables if necessary.

❧ For maximum nutritional value, prepare vegetables just before cooking and serve them as soon as they are cooked.

❧ Remember the smaller you cut vegetables the quicker the cooking time. For example, grated carrot will cook more quickly than carrot cut into slices.

❧ As a general guide when preparing and cooking vegetables remember: minimum water, minimum cooking and minimum cutting. Following this guide ensures that your vegetables retain maximum flavour, nutrients and vitamins. Vitamins such as vitamin C, folic acid and other B group vitamins are destroyed by heat and exposure to air, and they dissolve readily in cooking water. Steaming or microwaving are ideal cooking methods for retaining vitamins, flavour and texture.

The Right Size

What is the difference between cubed and diced vegetables or grated and sliced? The picture below the following guide will ensure that you prepare your vegetables correctly and so achieve the best results.

Cube: Cut into about 1 cm/½ in pieces.

Dice: Cut into 5 mm/¼ in pieces.

Mince: Cut into 3 mm/⅛ in pieces.

Grate: Use either a hand grater or a food processor with a grating attachment.

Slice: Cut either very thin or thick. You can also slice into rings. Another way to slice is to cut diagonally. This is a good way to prepare vegetables such as carrots, celery and zucchini (courgettes) for stir-frying.

Vegetable Preparation and Cooking Chart

VEGETABLE	PREPARATION	FREEZING
ARTICHOKES	Place upside down in salted water to dislodge any hidden insects or earth. Trim stem and tough outer leaves. Snip sharp points from leaves. Brush any cut surfaces with lemon juice to prevent discolouration.	Remove tough outer leaves, trim and remove choke. Blanch 7 minutes in water with lemon juice. Drain upside down. Pack in rigid containers.
ASPARAGUS	Bend lower end of stalk between thumb and forefinger to break off woody end.	Blanch 2-4 minutes, depending on thickness of stalk. Pack between sheets of freezer wrap.
BEANS – GREEN BEANS, RUNNER BEANS	All beans need to be topped and tailed, some varieties, such as runner beans, will also need their strings removed. Beans can then be sliced or left whole.	Blanch 2-3 minutes. Pack in freezer bags.
BEANS – BROAD BEANS	Cooking times for broad beans are very dependent on age and size. If young and using whole, wash, cut off ends and remove strings. Older beans should be shelled.	Blanch 1-2 minutes. Pack in freezer bags.
BEETROOT	Trim tops, leaving 5 cm to prevent 'bleeding' during cooking. Scrub gently with a soft brush.	Blanch 5-10 minutes. Peel and pack in freezer bags.
BROCCOLI	Trim tough woody stems, divide into florets. Rinse in cold water.	Blanch 3-4 minutes. Pack in layers between sheets of freezer wrap.
BRUSSELS SPROUTS	Trim base and tough outer leaves, do not trim too closely or the sprouts will fall apart during cooking.	Blanch 2-3 minutes. Pack in freezer bags.
CABBAGE	Trim tough and damaged outer leaves. Rinse, chop or shred.	Blanch 1 minute. Pack in freezer bags.
CARROTS	Top, tail and scrub – young carrots do not require peeling. Slice, dice, or cut into thin strips. Leave young carrots whole.	Blanch 3-5 minutes. Pack in freezer bags.
CAULIFLOWER	Remove leaves, rinse, leave whole or cut into florets.	Blanch 3 minutes. Pack into freezer bags or in rigid containers between sheets of freezer wrap.
CELERY	Separate stalks, trim top and base. Some varieties will require the strings to be removed, this is easily done using a vegetable peeler.	Blanch 2 minutes. Pack in freezer bags.

Cooking Methods and Times			
STEAM	**BOIL** *(Bring water to boil before adding vegetables.)*	**BAKE/ROAST** *(At 180°C/350°F/Gas 4 unless otherwise stated.)*	**MICROWAVE** *(Cook vegetables on HIGH (100%) and always cover before microwaving.)*
45 minutes or until fork easily pierces just above the base	30-45 minutes or until a leaf pulls out easily	45-60 minutes	4 artichokes 7-9 minutes (stand 3-4 minutes before serving)
15 minutes. Tie in bundles and stand in 2 cm/$^{3}/_{4}$ in of water	8-10 minutes in boiling water		500 g/1 lb, 5-6 minutes (stand 3-4 minutes before serving)
15 minutes	8-10 minutes depending on age and size		500 g/1 lb, 8 minutes with $^{1}/_{2}$ cup/125 mL/4 fl oz water (stand 3-4 minutes before serving)
20-30 minutes – but cooking times depend on age and size	15-20 minutes		500 g/1 lb, 8-10 minutes with $^{1}/_{4}$ cup/60 mL/2 fl oz water
	30-40 minutes	In foil, 1-1$^{1}/_{2}$ hours at 200°C/400°F/Gas 6	500 g/1 lb, 15 minutes (stand 5 minutes before serving)
10-15 minutes	5-10 minutes		500 g/1 lb, 5 minutes
10-15 minutes	10 minutes		500 g/1 lb, 5-6 minutes
5-10 minutes	3-5 minutes		500 g/1 lb, 4-5 minutes
20-25 minutes	15-20 minutes		500 g/ 1 lb, 8-10 minutes
10-15 minutes	8-10 minutes		500 g/1 lb, 6-8 minutes
10-15 minutes	5 minutes		500 g/1 lb, 4-5 minutes

VEGETABLE	PREPARATION	FREEZING
EGGPLANT (AUBERGINE)	Remove stem, halve, slice or dice. Place in colander and sprinkle with salt, leave 20 minutes, rinse and pat dry.	Cut into slices. Blanch 4 minutes and pack in rigid containers.
FENNEL	Trim root and top leaves, remove and discard any discoloured outer sheaths. Halve or slice.	Blanch 3 minutes. Pack in rigid container in blanching water.
LEEKS	Trim roots and tops. Rinse well to remove any earth between the leaves, leave whole or slice.	
MUSHROOMS	Wipe with a damp cloth. Wild mushrooms may need to be lightly rinsed and peeled.	Slice finely. Blanch 1-2 minutes and pack in freezer bags.
ONIONS	Remove skins and tough outer layers. Halve, quarter, dice or slice.	Chop, double wrap and pack in freezer bags.
PEAS	Shell and rinse.	Blanch 1 minute. Pack in freezer bags.
PEPPERS	Cut off top, remove seeds and core. Cube, dice or slice.	Halve, slice or dice. Blanch halves 3 minutes, sliced or diced 1½ minutes.
POTATOES – NEW	Wash and scrape with a small vegetable knife.	Blanch 4 minutes. Pack in freezer bags.
POTATOES – OLD	Wash, scrub and peel if desired. Leave whole, cut into halves or quarters.	Blanch 5 minutes. Pack in freezer bags.
PUMPKIN	Wash, cut into medium pieces. Remove seeds and skin if desired.	Cut into serving size pieces. Pack in freezer bags.
SILVERBEET	Separate white stem from green leaves. Shred leaves and cut stems into pieces.	Remove stalks. Blanch 2 minutes. Squeeze out as much liquid as possible and pack in freezer bags.
SNOW PEAS (MANGETOUT)	Top and tail. Remove strings.	Blanch 1 minute. Pack in freezer bags.
SPINACH	Cut off roots and stems. Remove any wilted or damaged leaves. Wash well in several changes of water.	Blanch 2 minutes. Squeeze out as much moisture as possible and pack in freezer bags.
SWEET CORN	If leaving husk on for cooking, gently pull back husk, remove silk, wash and pull husk back around the cob. Or husk can be completely removed before cooking.	Blanch 3-5 minutes. Wrap individually and pack in freezer bags.
ZUCCHINI (COURGETTE)	Wash and trim ends. Leave whole or cut into halves or slices.	Cut into slices. Blanch 2 minutes. Pack in freezer bags.

Cooking Methods and Times			
STEAM	**BOIL** *(Bring water to boil before adding vegetables.)*	**BAKE/ROAST** *(At 180°C/350°F/Gas 4 unless otherwise stated.)*	**MICROWAVE** *(Cook vegetables on HIGH (100%) and always cover before microwaving.)*
		45-60 minutes	500 g/1 lb, 5-8 minutes
15-20 minutes	10-15 minutes		500 g/1 lb, 5-6 minutes
15-20 minutes	10-15 minutes		500 g/1 lb, 5-6 minutes
			500 g/1 lb, 4-5 minutes
20-30 minutes	20-30 minutes	45-60 minutes	500 g/1 lb, 6-8 minutes
15-20 minutes	10-15 minutes		500 g/1 lb, 4-5 minutes
		When stuffed, 30-45 minutes	
25-30 minutes	15-25 minutes	30-45 minutes	500 g/1 lb, 8-10 minutes (stand 3-4 minutes before serving)
30-45 minutes	25-40 minutes	45 minutes-1$^1/_4$ hours	500 g/1 lb, 10-12 minutes (stand 3-4 minutes before serving)
35-45 minutes	20-30 minutes	45-60 minutes	500 g/1 lb, 10 minutes
10-15 minutes	5-10 minutes		500 g/1 lb, 4-5 minutes
5-10 minutes	3-5 minutes		500 g/1 lb, 3-4 minutes
10-15 minutes	5-10 minutes		500 g/1 lb, 4-5 minutes
	10-20 minutes		Each cob 2-3 minutes
5-10 minutes	5-10 minutes		500 g/1 lb, 4-5 minutes

INDEX

UK COOKERY EDITOR
Katie Swallow

EDITORIAL
Food Editor: Rachel Blackmore
Editorial Assistant: Ella Martin
Editorial Coordinator: Margaret Kelly
Recipe Development: Sheryle Eastwood, Lucy Kelly, Donna Hay, Anneka Mitchell, Penelope Peel, Belinda Warn, Loukie Werle
Credits: Recipe page 66 by June Budgen; page 67 by Lorna Rhodes; pages 68, 70 and 71 by Louise Steele © Merehurst Limited

COVER
Photography: Ashley Mackevicius
Styling: Wendy Berecry

PHOTOGRAPHY
Ashley Mackevicius, Harm Mol, Yanto Noerianto, Andy Payne, Jon Stewart, Warren Webb

STYLING
Wendy Berecry, Belinda Clayton, Rosemary De Santis, Carolyn Fienberg, Jacqui Hing, Michelle Gorry

DESIGN AND PRODUCTION
Manager: Sheridan Carter
Layout: Lulu Dougherty
Finished Art: Stephen Joseph
Design: Frank Pithers

Published by J.B. Fairfax Press Pty Limited
A.C.N. 003 738 430
Formatted by J.B. Fairfax Press Pty Limited
Printed by Toppan Printing Co, Hong Kong

JBFP 206 UK
Includes Index
ISBN 1 86343 102 0

Distributed by J.B. Fairfax Press Ltd
9 Trinity Centre, Park Farm Estate
Wellingborough, Northants, UK
Ph: (0933) 402330 Fax: (0933) 402234